The Authentic

By

Hannah Beko

authentically

Terms and Conditions

LEGAL NOTICE

By reading this document, the reader agrees under no circumstances is the author responsible for any losses, direct or indirect, that are incurred as a result of the use of the information contained within this document, including, but not limited to, errors, omissions, or inaccuracies.

Published by Babysteps Publishing Limited All enquires to kevin@babystepspublishing.com

ISBN-13 9798826226957

Table of Contents

Praise For This Book 7

Why I Wrote This Book? 13

Why Should You Read This Book?........................... 15

Chapter 1: Confidence.. 17

Chapter 2: Authenticity 45

Chapter 3: Character traits of Lawyers 77

Chapter 4: Tools of Effectiveness. 97

Chapter 5: Goals, Vision and Direction. 121

Chapter 6: Culture in Law. 135

Chapter 7: Mental Health in Law..............................155

Chapter 8: Men and Women in Law..........................167

Chapter 9: Leaders in Law..187

Chapter 10: Change and the Future 195

About the Author...207

Other Books and Services by the Author 209

Praise For This Book

It was so relevant and interesting to read. I just know this book will go such a long way to helping many lawyers in the profession feel that they are not alone in how they feel day to day! It really helps to highlight issues that so many of us experience (yet don't always admit) - there has never been a better time to live/be your authentic self!

It's not only super helpful but relevant, understandable, and relatable. I really like the use of questions. Powerful questions really get us thinking and help us create the necessary time to think.

I cannot tell you how much a book like this is NEEDED in the legal profession - I hope many legal professionals go out and buy it!

Suzanne Brimer, Commercial Litigation Solicitor

I love this book! The opening is super vulnerable and sets up the foundation for the rest.

The section on confidence is amazing and something I WISH I had seen about ten years ago.

I often buy non-fiction books because I like the subject matter and then struggle to read them. With this book, while I only jumped in and out, every section that I read drew me in.

Kate Sherburn, Head of Legal at Who Gives a Crap

Reading this book was an enlightening experience and so much resonated with me as a lawyer.

What makes this different from other books in this genre is how it genuinely and effectively changed my mindset, as well as assisted me with creating the framework to implement this change. Thanks, Hannah!

Caroline Harrington, Private Client Lawyer

A must-read! Hannah is a fine example of how to embrace being your true authentic self in the workplace. Hannah is one of a kind, showcased by how much she does to give back to the legal profession! Not only has Hannah propelled to success sitting as one of the most prominent property partners in the UK, but she also works as a coach and trainer to the legal profession, speaking out on important areas such as mental health and happiness in law and all her resources are of the highest quality – most notably of course The Authentic Lawyer, which is a real masterpiece!

I also love what Hannah has done with her Lawyers Business Mastermind Group, which brings together legal business owners, self-employed lawyers, and consultants, providing a platform for entrepreneurial lawyers to grow! Hannah's 'Build Your Legal Business' podcast, aimed at lawyers who want to scale out without burning out, is fantastic! With all this wisdom and know-how, I couldn't have thought of anybody better in the legal profession to have authored this superb book! Highly recommend!

Robert Hanna - Founder of KC Partners & Host of Legally Speaking Podcast

This book is such a relevant and easy read. It hits the spot and will resonate with so many. Hannah has really managed to distil such a loaded discourse with hard-hitting, punchy content.

Somaya Ouazzani, founder of specialist legal recruitment consultancy Mimosa Fleur

I have watched Hannah develop her ideas about authenticity over the last five years or so, both while we worked together and afterward. This book needed to be written and written by someone who is practicing law at the same time.

It has a lot of useful ideas and "thinking" information. I didn't agree with all of it, but it did make me think about all sorts of things-- and in the widest possible context-- in my role as a lawyer.

I hope this book gets the widespread coverage it deserves.

Nick Gould, common sense, corporate, deal-making and business lawyer for over 35 years.

W hat an incredible book. A must-have for all lawyers. The author's deep understanding of what it is like to be a lawyer and the pressures that are inherent in the industry comes across in a way that is knowledgeable and easy to implement. The author tackles difficult mental well-being, confidence, and the leadership skills required in a powerful and yet simple way, which is a real talent. Stress and burnout are widespread in the legal industry, and it is often expected to be part and parcel of the job.

The Authentic Lawyer is a legal handbook that needs to be on the reading list on day 1 of law school. A brilliant achievement.

Adele Stickland, Wellness in the workplace Resilience Trainer & ICF Coach

Why I Wrote This Book?

I can remember vividly the moment I decided to write this book in 2015. Driving home in my shiny new red car, trying not to have a panic attack, repeatedly asking God to let me be grateful one day for what I was going through. And... knowing at that moment that I would record what I'd learned for others to benefit from, so perhaps they could avoid the place I'd found myself in.

Authentically Speaking (my training and coaching consultancy for lawyers) was born from one frightening statistic. In 2015 the Law Society surveyed over 8,500 lawyers, and **95% reported suffering from moderate to severe work-related stress**. I wasn't alone, but I was angry and sad. As a result of my own chronic stress, I went on to discover just how widespread and, at the time, unspoken the issue was in law.

A fellow commercial property partner told me (when I explained my plans for Authentically Speaking) that stress was just part and parcel of the job. It was something we all just needed to accept. He then went on to spend an hour telling me about the most stressful times in his career and how so many of his decisions in the latter part were driven by those negative experiences. Far from putting me off from my new business venture, he proved my point that something needed to change!

I had created my second business and had a third son by this stage! After a much-needed heart-to-heart with my wonderful friend Adele Stickland, I realised I needed to put the book down for a while. Writing began in 2019 with all intentions of being finished by August that year. Then as everyone knows, the world changed in March 2020.

In some ways, the legal profession as we knew it has changed as a result of the global pandemic - as have many of the lawyers I was writing this book for. I have endeavoured to bring the contents up to date, but please forgive me for any references which might be a little "pre-pandemic" but I hope still relevant.

Why Should You Read This Book?

Over the past few years, I've coached and trained thousands of lawyers and continued to work inside my own commercial property practice.

Alongside the practical coaching and training, I love researching what makes us lawyers tick. Why we think, act and feel the way we do, why we suffer from stress more than the general population, and why we leave (or consider leaving) the profession we trained for so long to join.

When I created my second business, I knew I'd need practical support, tools, and guidance from others who had walked the path before me. Aside from extra business skills, I've learned on that journey that is just how much we aren't taught as lawyers - that would be REALLY useful for our careers and practices.

Inside this book, you will learn valuable business skills and life and career hacks that can have a huge impact on your levels of satisfaction, success, and enjoyment!

Like you, I suspect, I worked hard from a young age to get the grades for University, a good degree, into my first firm, and then to qualify as a solicitor. By the age of 35, I had the title "partner," a successful practice, a new house, and a new red shiny car. I "should" have been really grateful.

When I realised all of the achievement and box-ticking didn't make me happy, I threw out the rulebook and started a new one. In some ways, this book is a codified version of that rulebook. I will try to share with you the lessons, tools, and exercises that made a huge difference to me.

You will also find additional resources on the accompanying website www.theauthenticlawyer.com.

So if you're a practicing member of the legal profession and/or if you lead and manage other legal professionals and want to get the very best from them, grab a drink and sit down with a pen (if you don't like writing inside books, a notepad) and let's dive in...

Chapter 1

Confidence

66

"Because one believes in oneself,
one doesn't try to convince
others. Because one is content
with oneself, one doesn't need
others' approval. Because one
accepts oneself, the whole world
accepts him or her."

— LAO TZU

Confidence (Cambridge Dictionary):
The quality of being certain of your abilities or of
having trust in people, plans, or the future.

How often do we hear that what so and so needs is to have more confidence?

Whether it's a job interview, handling a file on their own, learning to delegate, applying for a promotion, delivering a pitch, interacting with other teams, or leading a practice group, these activities require confidence.

There is also the confidence required to approach your line manager if you need to take time off, return to work after a break, or request part-time work as a man when no one else in your team works that way.

As a lawyer's coach, I'm regularly asked by firms to support senior people in increasing their confidence. I've worked with clients ranging from paralegals to managing partners on similar issues.

A lack of confidence is often what stops us from doing, saying, or being what it is that we need to in that moment.

Why is confidence so important?

Do people tell you that you should have more confidence in yourself or in your abilities?
Do you ever say to yourself, "If I had more confidence, I would..." (you fill in the blank)?
Is a lack of confidence stopping you from moving forward in your life and career?

The following are examples of where I commonly see lawyers struggling with confidence:

1. Not going for an internal promotion because they don't feel ready, or they perceive themselves to be not as good as Joe Bloggs.
2. Not applying for jobs externally, not feeling qualified enough, or not able to leave their current position because they've been there a while and feel it would be disloyal. They have it good there.
3. Not stepping up to lead a team or project when really they are more than qualified and would quite like to try.
4. Not standing up to a demanding client who imposes a deadline because it suits them, rather than it being a genuine and reasonable timeframe.

5. Not standing up to an overdemanding boss.

6. Not speaking out in team meetings about changes they want to see, unfair behaviour or treatment that is bothering them, or highlighting their own achievements in front of others.

7. Not getting visible, hiding their light under a bushel rather than letting people know about a client win, great feedback they've received, or perhaps a team result they've produced.

8. Working to "wrote," i.e., the trap of presenteeism. Feeling the need to be in the office for the "contracted hours" when it might suit them to come in later or to leave earlier for one reason or another. (I'm certain the vast majority of diligent lawyers reading this book are highly likely to work far in excess of their contracted hours!)

Two types of confidence

Outer Confidence

I'm sure we can all think of the loudest person in our team or office. They probably take over the team or client meetings, speaking the longest, but often without saying a great deal by way of substance. This is what I am referring to in relation to outward confidence.

These individuals might be labelled as confident people, and anyone measuring themselves against that person is likely to feel that they lack the same levels of confidence. But outer confidence can be a show or a demonstration that hides an inner feeling of lack of confidence. It can be a protective mechanism or perhaps a learnt behaviour following a role model or senior leader who acts in a similar way.

What fascinates me when we see this sort of person is whether they genuinely have higher levels of confidence than others or whether they are displaying behaviour they think they should and inside feel far from confident. I'm always interested in why we act the way we do!

Inner Confidence

On the other hand, inner confidence can be quietly spoken unless the need arises to be louder. Inner confidence doesn't always need a lot of words or to take over in meetings. They can get their point across swiftly and succinctly without "fluff" or unnecessary verbiage.

Silence can be a powerful tool in making your point. If you stay quiet and listen, then hit them with your point swiftly and simply; this can work very effectively. As a young litigator, I used this in a negotiation meeting to get exactly what our client wanted, and I've been using it ever since.

After a very protracted lease renewal (I won't bore the non-property lawyers with the details), we had a final face-to-face meeting before proceeding to court. The lawyer on the other side talked... a lot. I sat quietly, listening to what he had to say. I did worry that my client might think, "what are we paying her for, to sit there and not say anything." But I tried the silent approach anyway.

The solicitor got everything off his chest and set out his client's demands. Once he'd finished, I pointed out that he wouldn't get what he was demanding and suggested something else instead if we went to court. I remember the client commenting afterward on what a difficult person the other side had been and how well I'd handled it.

I didn't stay in litigation, but I think the approach can be useful in many situations, including handling upset or frustrated clients. Often what most people need is just to be able to say their piece and to be heard. If we have the confidence to sit back and let them "vent," as it were, we can hit them with our position swiftly and succinctly. I use the same approach in board meetings, panel discussions, and even coaching sessions!

In meetings or even in pitches, it can be tempting to be the person who speaks the most. To let your client see you "performing" because they are paying you well. For some practice areas or in some situations, I appreciate sometimes this may be necessary. All I want personally is the best outcome for my client, as simply and smoothly as possible; it works pretty well by letting the other side talk, nod and smile, then offer what we are happy to offer.

We don't need to be the loudest person in the room or the person who uses the most words to get our point across. Less is more, and confidence exudes from someone who isn't afraid of the silence rather than talking a lot without saying a great deal. The "empty can rattles the most" after all!

Less is more

It takes inner confidence to make things simple. So much in law has been about the profession being different, special. In the "old days," lawyers were revered, and perhaps we've been living up to that by using complicated technical jargon when a few simple words would have done the job.

I don't know about you, but I can say I've ever felt revered in my career, and I think those days are long gone. My farmer grandmother was most disappointed when I became a lawyer and asked me why I couldn't do something useful, like be a vet!

My commercial and personal clients want a straight-talking, easy-to-understand lawyer who understands what they are trying to achieve and does their best to deliver it as simply as possible. That's what they tell me anyway.

I encourage you to favour developing a true sense of inner confidence rather than putting on the "character armour" of outer confidence. I say develop because this is a muscle that grows with time and practice. It takes time and commitment but can definitely be done. The tools and exercises in this book will help.

Authenticity and Confidence

I'm often asked about the interlink between authenticity and confidence; are they the same thing?

I don't agree they are the same, but they can walk alongside each other. As a legal business owner, I wouldn't have necessarily said I had confidence issues, but looking back now, after I ventured into embracing my own authenticity, my confidence has moved to an entirely different level. It isn't just confidence in my work but in every area of life. As a mother, as a speaker, an author, a coach, and **a** trainer.

As we become more of our authentic selves, we increase our inner confidence. I believe that authenticity grows first, and inner confidence grows alongside it.

Effective delegation and empowering others

The old adage that lawyers were trained as lawyers and not as managers remain true, although this is changing as new generations of managers are coming through. More team leaders and managers are coming for training and coaching through their firms or even investing themselves, wanting to be the best they can be.

Learning to delegate effectively and making those we delegate feel empowered is key for running any team or business. We were taught to review caselaw, draft documents, and interview clients.

In the firms I've worked **in**, we weren't taught to "share" work or to ask for help by delegating to others when we had a lot on our plate, even if someone else was quieter. That might have been over **ten** years ago, but I still hear of teams where one person is almost burned out, and the person sitting next to them is worried about being made redundant!

If and when you move into a managerial role, even if you are an NQ supervising a paralegal or secretary, how can you delegate more effectively?

Can you identify what stops you from delegating?

I've interviewed lawyers about what stops them from delegating as much as they could and working with coaching clients who may be heads of departments or even the law firm owners. Why don't they delegate as much as they should?

Reasons include, this job isn't a very good or interesting one, my assistant won't want to do it (but you as a head of a department should be doing it?), it will take me too long to explain what needs to be done, (but if we don't take the time to train others up, we will be forever doing it), if I delegate this and they don't do it well I will need to redo it anyway.

Behind all these reasons, I hear fear. Fear of losing time if it takes too long or needs redoing. Fear of judgment if they are better than me, fear they will be disengaged and leave if I give them boring or menial work to do.

When I raise delegation with lawyers, they often share stories about their own time recording and billing, keeping them stuck in overwork and not saying no. I say stories because this is what they are, stories that we tell ourselves. This frame of mind only leads to longer and longer hours and more exhaustion. It takes that inner confidence to know that you are worthy of support and assistance from those around you.

Another "favourite" fear of mine around delegation is this "If I delegate this and they do a good job, they might have my job!". Again, this keeps us in overwhelm with too much to do. What if, instead, we said, "if I delegate this and they do a good job, I've done a good job in training them and supporting them to do well." Doesn't that feel better, like the makings of a more productive team, and actually encourages effective delegation? This way of thinking takes inner confidence and self-esteem, which is another reason it is so important to take the time to develop this skill.

If you want to move into higher management (or are already there), it is key to delegate effectively and help your people feel empowered and confident in themselves. Holding too tightly onto control (another sign of an inner confidence gap) does not empower your team to be the best they can possibly be for you, themselves, and the firm.

Note: empowering doesn't look like "dumping" something on someone and seeing if they sink or swim like when we started out. Just because it happened it us doesn't mean we should perpetuate the disempowering treatment. The stress of a lack of supervision and support when needed leads to underdeveloped juniors, a lack of useful and well-trained resources for you, and mental health struggles for the team.

Fear of failure, of getting it wrong

I bet most people looking into our profession from the outside would assume that lawyers exude confidence. Ally McBeal and Suits show us, lawyers, as confidence personified! The reality is that the journey into a legal career equips us with an amazing suit of "character armour" and some great "masks."

The archetype of a lawyer could be recognised easily. If you ask people in any language or culture, "what does a lawyer look and sound like? What character traits do they have?" I expect you'd have similar responses.

We find ourselves doing our best to live up to the list of expectations, even down to the "uniform" black suit (or similar). Perhaps you have to be inside the profession to understand the fear of failure and of getting it wrong.

We're trained to be good analysers and problem solvers, to look for all the things that could go wrong and draft ways to avoid them. We always look for the worst-case scenario; we expect the worst. We look for where the other side is trying to "get one over" on our clients or us. It's perhaps little wonder that we are so fearful of getting it wrong.

If you believe the rhetoric and increasing anecdotal evidence, the tide may be changing with the millennials and gen z, but not for those of us on the more senior side. Add the fact that lawyers train hard for years and face huge competition for training contracts (or pupillages). It's highly competitive once you're inside as well for those highly coveted senior positions. (We will consider this further in the Future of the Law Chapter).

Lawyers are high achievers. We were probably all high achievers from a young age. For my own part, I know the day it began. I was eight years old and had a spelling test at school. I returned home pleased that I'd scored 9 out of 10. This probably tells you that my early nature was not that of a perfectionist! My Dad (also one of my greatest supporters) said, "that's great, but what happened to the other one?".

That day a perfectionist was born. My Dad wanted me to be the very best I could be. He knew that I could be at the top academically with hard work, and he wanted, as so many parents of that generation did, for us to be the best we could be.

Perhaps you can relate; maybe you have your own version of the story that created your inner high achiever? I'm not suggesting that we blame our parents (or anyone else) for doing the very best they could with the knowledge they had at the time. They wanted us to have the best possible education and chances in life. When we achieved, they were proud of us. We soon decided as children (completely unconsciously, of course) that achievement was welcomed and celebrated and something to strive for.

In whatever way it was created, this inner high achiever is a large part of the reason we fear failure or getting it wrong. We'd probably always been top of the class at school and throughout our education years, and suddenly in law, we're surrounded by others just as bright (or maybe even brighter). It's even harder to stay at the top. But, we should recognise the high achiever in us and see where it can stop us from being happy and potentially (and ironically) even hold us back in our careers.

I'm certainly no parenting or child education expert, but when my then eight-year-old son came home and told me he'd scored 8 out of 10 on his spelling test, I had to think very hard about what to say. I wanted to reply with something suitably encouraging but not diminish his achievement.

I certainly knew what I wasn't going to say. In the end, I went with, *"that's great. Do you remember the words we need to learn, and we can have a look at them"*? His reply, "*I think 8 out of 10 is quite good*," still humbles my once very unhappy high achiever, and I agreed with him that it was.

Our lawyer perfectionist tendencies, whilst making us good document reviewers and drafters, can also lead us to feel that nothing we do is good enough, ultimately that we aren't good enough. This path doesn't lead anywhere except exhaustion and fleeting moments of happiness. No achievement is enough; there is always more.

Let's deal with the final reason I believe we fear failure.

Claims.

Perhaps our worst nightmare? We catastrophise over it. We believe a claim will end our career, and we'll lose our jobs, our clients, and our reputation. Very rarely is this true? But it's the story we tell ourselves.

I'm forever grateful to the lawyers who have willingly shared their experiences of claims to show that there certainly is life afterward, and if it gives you comfort, I've heard it said that you aren't a proper lawyer until you've dealt with a claim!

Letting go of expectations

If we understand where our high achieving tendencies originate from and why we have such a fear of failure, what's next? I'd advocate that it's time to start letting go of some of the high expectations we have of ourselves.

It's okay not to be perfect (honestly, it is).
It's okay to fail.
FAIL – First Attempt In Learning
FAIL – Found Another Interesting Lesson

I encourage you to see anything that doesn't go exactly as you'd like it to – as something to learn from. When we look for the lessons in life, nothing is truly bad – it's happened for a reason. The reason we can't always see at the time but looking back, we can connect the dots. Maybe you didn't get a promotion or a job you've applied for. Maybe you didn't win a big pitch you'd put your heart and soul into. What did you learn? What would you do or not do next time?

Be kinder to yourself. Realise that high achievers left unchecked can make for fairly unhappy people on one side of the scale, and it's a short slope towards anxiety and depression.

Overachievers never stop. No achievement is large enough; you're never "done," and no number of ticked boxes makes you feel fulfilled. You will always be striving for more, for the next big thing. Some may disagree with me and take the view that we should always be working towards something.

But I question whether sometimes what we should be spending a little time on might be our own sense of peace. Contentment with where we are at present.

Spending time with our family and friends. Maybe we can redirect some of that overachiever energy into something we've always wanted to do. Perhaps taking up a new sport or hobby?

I've spent the last seven years studying and training in techniques to increase happiness and reduce stress. When I started, I never once thought that my business and my life would change completely in pursuing this. I redirected my overachiever tendencies into wanting to find a way to be happy.

Let's say you took up a new sport or hobby for the sake of your health or just for enjoyment and relaxation. You would meet new people. Those people would get to know you and then discover what you do for a living. They would get the chance to know like and trust you on a personal level. When they need a lawyer – chances are they will come to you. Perhaps it's your specialist area; perhaps it's a colleague or a friend. It doesn't matter who the work goes to if you believe in business karma, it will come back to you!

I've been a bit of an amateur property investor since my 20s and, over the last few years, picked up this passion again by joining property investment groups and trainings. I volunteer to deliver some of the training - I will stand up and talk about just about anything, as you'll see in the Authenticity chapter!

Initially, I'd spend two days with a group of property investors before some of them discovered I was also a property lawyer in the "day job." They started referring work to me and recommending me to other networking group members. This has been my main source of business development for a long time, and it was an accident that came about after following my own interests in property!

Let yourself rest. Spend time enjoying your life, your family, home, and children. These may be the best years of your life. No doubt you've heard the saying that on your death bed, you are not going to wish you'd spent more time at work; you'll more likely wish you spent more time with your loved ones and doing things you enjoy.

I refer to the writing of Bronnie Ware in "*The Top Five Regrets of the Dying*," a palliative care nurse who recorded the biggest regrets of her patients in their final weeks of life. She found that we tend to regret the things we didn't do, not the things we did. The top regret, especially from men, "I wish I hadn't worked so hard."

Try to remember this as often as you can. Perhaps put-up post-it notes or send yourself diary reminders. Keep putting work into perspective, and then do it again and again whenever you lose touch.

Please don't think this is me recommending that you "check out." That you give up on ambition – whatever that means to you. I consider myself very ambitious, certainly more so now than ever. But achievement doesn't have to be so hard or with quite so many sacrifices.

We only get one life, and we must take time to smell the roses. We must sometimes contract to expand, which I take to mean that pushing gets us to exhaustion, burnt out, and opting out.

Rest, recuperate and recharge when you need to (making time to enjoy your life) and you will soar, I promise!

Confidence comes from knowing yourself

If confidence is key, just how do we get or increase it. That's the million-dollar question. Whilst it might be true that so and so just needs to have more confidence, just telling someone they need to have more confidence doesn't really help. It's a neat way for them to blame themselves for why they didn't get that promotion or pay rise or weren't given the extra responsibility or the autonomy they were looking for.

You can't nip to Tesco (or Waitrose if that's your thing) and pick it up. You can buy a book like this about confidence but (and I realise I'm shooting myself in the foot here) on its own, that book isn't going to help you improve your confidence.

I will share how you can do this with me, and I hope you will take up the challenge. These strategies take work. It's not a magic bullet or a piece of information you can learn, and that's it.

Confidence is a feeling; it's a way of being. Inner confidence comes from really knowing yourself and your place in the world. It's becoming comfortable with who you are. It's not being paralysed by fear of failing in some way, preventing you from moving forward in your career.

In the next chapter (Authenticity), we will delve into how you can look at knowing yourself better. It's not about becoming someone else, emulating your boss or another successful figure in your life - that's the outer confidence we talked about earlier in the chapter.

Outer confidence is the armour, the pretence. People can see through it. It's temporary, it's tiring, and it's not authentic. This is about re-discovering who you really are and learning to live it more and more each day.

Other tips for increasing confidence

Having a brag jar

I'll be talking about "showing off" in the next chapter. After reading a LinkedIn post about how lawyers "should" be humble and not shout about their client wins but be quietly proud of their accomplishments, I had to hold my tongue. Although I have a lot of respect for the author of this post, I completely disagree. We've heard this rubbish for too long.

We should not be arrogant or big-headed, rude, or trample over others. But we do need to be proud of our accomplishments and be ready and willing to stick our heads above the parapet to say when we're really pleased with what we've achieved.

When you receive praise from a client, do you keep it stored somewhere? Can you screenshot it? If it's given verbally, can you put it down on email? Save the email in a "brag jar" email folder. This is great material for bringing out at appraisal time or for using in testimonials on your website or pitch documents.

Another good use for the brag jar is to pull this out when you feel your confidence dip. Remind yourself of the good things others have to say about you.

Join a friendly networking group

Having the support of others is so important. Knowing that others feel the same as you, or who can listen to how you're feeling and understand, makes a big difference.

I'd like to share the story of one of our Women Lawyers and Mothers Group members.

> **Alyah had returned to work after an extended period of maternity leave about 6 months prior to us meeting. She was already feeling bored and no longer challenged in her role and wanted to move up in her firm. But she felt that her absence of almost 2 years and relatively short time since returning, would mean she wasn't eligible for consideration.**
>
> **Initially a lack of confidence in her own abilities prevented her from even having the conversation at work. She later told me that after two meetings of our networking group she felt confident enough to apply for the position and was successful. Seeing other women in the group progressing and going for promotions, she asked her herself, "why not me?"**

My favourite part of her feedback was that even just walking into the room; she felt that she stood a little taller. A couple of years later, in a workshop I held on goal setting and planning, she shared her latest dream of pursuing a judicial post. She's working towards that now.

Men, Women, and Confidence

We can't move on from the confidence discussion without tackling the potential elephant in the room. Statistically and anecdotally, women are said to be less confident than men. It's a reason often touted for the difference in promotion prospects between men and women and the gender pay gap. Women returning from maternity leave are so often considered to have suffered a crisis in confidence, or they persuade themselves that they have!

We will talk more about the differences between men and women in Chapter 8. Yes, I want to acknowledge that women tend statistically to have more of an issue with confidence than men.

But I also work with men who are suffering from a lack of confidence. This could often be due to events such as illness, time away from work, bullying, or maybe making a mistake. Even just starting something new, a new role or position that takes some getting used to, is outside of their comfort zone. These things shake confidence whether they are men or women. While proportionally more women struggle with low confidence, it might well be that the traits bringing us into the law (examined further in Chapter 3) result in both men and women tackling this issue.

I hope you find these chapters useful, even if as a window or insight into how others in your team or organisation might be feeling and how you can support them.

Adrian Barker, Global L&D Manager at Freshfields told me...

Throughout my time as an executive coach, I have found confidence and the lack of it, to be the single greatest inhibitor to anyone's long term success. Being a lawyer is such a reputational existence, you trade on your brand and your reputation and anything that might remove the veneer of that public facing persona is often dismissed by the individual in favour of something more traditional, safer.

I have lost count of the amount of folk I have encountered that have been stuck and have felt lost in what would externally appear to be a successful career. It is often at this point they reach out for coaching and through the process we discover the decisions they have not taken and the risks they have avoided which have led to this malaise in their career paths. The what if's will get in your way if you allow them to, they will remove your edge and dampen your impact, so what to do!

As a coach I do not believe in being able to remove this professional self-doubt, what I do believe in is recognising where it exists, its impact and how to work with it rather than let it work you. Its not a quick process but coaching can help accelerate the progress you can make and help you to become self-sufficient in recognising and taming your own demons. I always ask...

What would happen if....?

What's the worst potential outcome...?

What have you got to lose...?

Ask yourself these questions about engaging in coaching and take back control of your career.

Chapter 2

Authenticity

"Authenticity is about being true
to who you are, even when
everyone around you wants you
to be someone else."

— MICHAEL JORDAN

Do you bring your whole self to work?

Or

When you transition from home to work mode, do you leave a part of yourself behind?

My "Authenticity as a Lawyer Superpower" presentation opens with my asking the audience these questions. On average, I've found that around half of the room believe they bring their whole self to work, and around half do not. There is a similar split between the men and women in the room.

As you dive further into this book, how much of the "authentic you" do you believe you bring into your work on a regular basis?

My aim is for you to consider how much more of your unique and fantastic self you can bring to your work in the future. You will not finish reading this book and walk into the office the next morning being 100% your authentic self; it's a journey, perhaps the journey of a career or a lifetime. My hope is that you decide it's worthwhile.

My journey of increasing authenticity

Here you see me in the middle of the picture, aged eight years old. I loved this pink My Little Pony tracksuit — it's become a highlight of my Authenticity presentations!

I introduce my 8-year-old self, other than to entertain people with my palm tree hairstyle, to illustrate the idea that children are generally 100% authentic. I say generally as there as occasions where this is not the case when traumatic childhoods are involved. Children don't have hang-ups about the world and about what people think about them.

They don't have the same fears that we do as we get older.

Around the ages of 7-8 years old, we develop our sense of awareness of our world. Before this age, children are only aware of themselves.

Put simply, they only care about themselves and what they like, don't like, and want to do! Young children will jump up on the table and dance; they'll sing in front of anyone who will listen and perform their plays. They don't give a second thought about what others think of them or whether they are any good at the activity they are undertaking. It doesn't even enter their heads to think, "what do people think about me?", "am I embarrassing myself here?" or "am I doing this right?".

In society, we create this sense of "embarrassing ourselves" by "boasting" or "showing off." My eldest son took the lead role in the school nativity for the first three years at school.

A few years ago, I asked him if he had put himself forward for the lead role, and he said he wanted to let someone else have a go; he didn't want to be seen to be "showing off." I hope these are not ideas I have instilled in him, as I've worked hard not to, but they are there anyway; it's in our society and culture.

I see this in my lawyer coaching clients. They come to work on (amongst other things) improving business development, picking up more clients, and improving their visibility and profile. They want to showcase their skills and talk about themselves. I can hear how uncomfortable they feel. As if sharing that glowing testimonial sounds like bragging or showing off.

These are feelings we've been brought up with, either directly within our families or simply through the culture, we're living in.

It doesn't help us to take the plunge and develop a great profile on LinkedIn, stand up at that pitch meeting, or walk confidently into a networking room and "be ourselves". Does that matter?

Yes.

All things being equal, people do business with and refer business to people they know, like, and trust."
(Networking and referral expert Bob Burg
"Endless Referrals")

People do business with those they know, like, and trust. Authentic people are easier to know, like, and trust.

We are our most authentic selves when young, that is until we take steps to consider this in adulthood, which I encourage you to do as you read this book.

As we get older, the world starts to impact us, and we start to worry about other people's judgment; we start to alter our behavior to fit in, to be accepted. This is a natural "animal" brain if you like. When humans evolved, if we didn't fit into the group or were ostracised for some reason, we would die.

Without realizing it, we are still driven by this primitive desire to fit in, to feel safe. This can butt up against our desire to be more authentic which carries the risk of us "standing out" – exactly the thing we need to do as lawyers to progress our careers and businesses!

I use the "palm tree hair" photograph as a reminder of the "identity" I had as a child. A fond memory of this time was hiring a very bulky video camera each summer. Every time the camera was turned on, I was in front of it! My parents tried to record my brother and sister's videos, and there I was front and centre, singing and dancing, delivering the six o'clock news, or interviewing Mopsey, the rabbit. It made for very uncomfortable viewing when I met my now-husband!

But something changed, and that girl disappeared. As I got older, the outside world started to impact me. My family moved from the South to the North of England, and I spent 18 months at a primary school where the school bullies instructed everyone not to speak to me; they didn't like my "posh" accent. I stopped putting my hand up, speaking up, and "showing off." I lost my authentic self for many years.

World-renowned coach Tony Robbins says, "change comes from inspiration or desperation," and in my case, it was chronic stress, the edge of burnout, and the beginnings of panic attacks – definitely desperation.

I started on a path toward the work I do now in 2015. An early part of that work (much more is covered inside the rest of this book) was taking a long look at who I was. Internally and externally, I would say, "I'm Hannah; I'm a lawyer." It had become my identity, perhaps my "character armour." I began asking myself that painful question: "other than a lawyer, who am I?"

A great coach suggested I look at who I was around six years of age. What was I like as a child? What did I love? And I realised, or rather remembered (after many tears), that I loved being in front of a camera. I loved presenting and speaking. That realisation was the start.

Within months (albeit shaking like a leaf), I began giving presentations, public speaking, writing, delivering training, and running workshops. I co-authored "Future Proof Your Legal Career" and "Effective Practice Group Leadership," published by Globe Law and Business, and delivered hundreds of hours of webinars, courses, and away days – it doesn't feel like work! Seven years on, I have trained and/or coached thousands of lawyers and legal business owners.

A favourite author of mine Gay Hendricks, in his book "*The Zone of Genius*," talks about uncovering the work we love to do that doesn't feel like work but which benefits the world.

Right now, this is it for me. I sometimes wonder whether I would have found it if I hadn't experienced the "rough patch" in 2015.

What is "Authentic"?

The term appeared in the English language about 500 years ago and meant "we all have our own path to tread." In the legal profession, we often get caught up on a conveyor belt of what is expected of us, what the career looks like, and what the career demands. It is a fantastic profession for mapping out what the future looks like, certainly at least for the early years. We don't always stop to think, *"what is it that my path looks like*?" But, unfortunately, conforming and fitting in with the group is easier and it is safer.

Talking about safety might seem a bit melodramatic, but psychological safety is what our brain is craving, and it's very clever in finding ways to get what it wants. Our mind will look for ways to take us away from situations or thoughts that leave us feeling threatened or unsafe, but it might be running on very old programming.

Suppose you consider our cave people ancestors. When our brains first developed, we were in danger if we didn't fit into the group; we could die if we were left outside of that group. Conforming and fitting in, being part of the group, became a life survival issue. Our brains haven't actually changed all that much, and when we feel we're different or outside the group, this triggers these feelings. Whether we realise it or not, it's the same part of the brain being activated, and we're afraid something terrible is going to happen. This is why it can be hard to be yourself, to feel that you stand out from other people because fitting in and conforming feels safer for that part of our brain.

In a profession like ours, we use what I frequently refer to as "*character armour*" out of fear that our peers might reject or ridicule us. This character armour is very evident in the law. You can easily picture the archetypal image of a lawyer; this is what lawyers look like, this is the way they talk, what they talk about, where they go on holiday, and what they wear. We have all these ideas about what a lawyer is; it's a very typical sort of character. We wear that armour to protect us from being rejected, and so we feel that we are accepted. We do this subconsciously often, without even realising.

In the early part of our careers, we role model our peers to try and understand how we're going to best fit into this career and to progress. To some extent (if you can find a role model you identify with), this is going to be a natural part of discovering who you are in the profession. But I urge you to consider finding the right time for you to move away from emulating a role model to becoming an authentic role model in your own right.

Self-awareness

Self-awareness, being aware of who we are, is a key part of our authenticity. In conducting the interviews for my contribution to "Effective Group Practice Leadership," I also discovered that self-awareness and authenticity are the key differentiators between excellent leaders and the not so brilliant ones.

What are your strengths and your limitations?

What do you love doing?

What do you dislike?

Who were you as a child before the world and it's expectations got hold of you?

Self-awareness involves the ability to analyse our thoughts, actions and feelings objectively. One simple but very effective process you can use to analyse thoughts and feelings is the cycle of thought creation. This is often one of the highlights of a training session when lawyers understand that they are actually in control of what they are thinking and feeling, far more so than they might initially believe.

Let's start with the following flow diagram demonstrating how our thoughts are created.

www.theauthenticlawyer.com

If we start at the top, we have a "*Moment*" or an "*Event*." This might be something very small, a comment or an email or a phone call.

Our brain gives this "*Moment*" a "*Meaning.*" The meaning we give to a particular moment or event is influenced by many factors including but not limited to:

Have we seen something similar before in our history, and what did it mean?

Our belief systems, the culture we grew up in.

Our own values and sense of what's important to us (refer to Chapter 4 on Tools of Effectiveness for more on Values).

Our body, are we tired, run-down, poorly, or had a recent argument with our other half?

Depending on the meaning we give to the moment dictates the emotions we subsequently feel.

The emotions we are feeling in this moment lead us to take certain actions.

Let's walk this process through by way of an example:

Moment = you are out for a meal with friends and leave the table to use the toilet. You return to the table, and everyone immediately stops talking.

What meaning do you give to this moment? What do you say to yourself that this means?
Do you believe that they were talking about you, perhaps not very pleasant, or they were talking about something they don't want you to hear?

What feelings would you have in this situation? Would you feel hurt, upset, paranoid, or mistrustful? Perhaps you'd feel detached or isolated as if everyone else is in on something you are not.

What actions would you take as a result of these feelings? Would you confront the group and question them? Perhaps you'd choose to leave early, to go home?

I use this process in workshops and receive a mixture of responses as to how you might feel in this situation and how you might react.

Let's examine the same moment in a different light.

Moment = you are out for a meal with friends and leave the table to go use the toilet. You return to the table and everyone immediately stops talking, but you know that you have a big birthday coming up in a month's time.

What meaning might you give to this moment now? Would you feel excited, special, valued, appreciated, happy, safe, and secure as a part of that friendship group?

What action might you take now? Choose to ignore the moment, not wanting them to have to spoil the surprise? You'd probably not sit there quietly brooding and then decide to leave early.

This cycle of thought process can be used in many situations, and I will refer to it in other chapters, but I use it here to encourage you to become more self-aware on your journey towards a more authentic you.

Take a pause when you encounter a moment that gives rise to certain feelings that you might consider uncomfortable (anger, sadness, jealousy, etc.).

Take a second or two to question the truth of the meaning you have given to that moment. Are you making assumptions, bringing in your past experiences, or telling yourself stories as to what the moment means?

Using this pause and reflecting on the truth of the meaning you are giving to the moment give you a chance to feel differently and react differently to a given situation. As we move towards authenticity, we can react less from a place of assumptions and old beliefs and more from a place of the present and what is true at the moment.

Handling emotions

Authentic lawyers are very aware of their emotions. We don't need to be afraid of them or push them down because they are uncomfortable or have what we'd label as negative emotions. Squashing down our emotions is probably something most human beings have become pretty good at, except perhaps Tibetan Monks or the Dali Lama.

We use comfort food, alcohol, binge-watching Netflix, and more to try and "avoid" uncomfortable emotions like shame, embarrassment, fear of failure, not being good enough, and not being able to handle it all.

Being able to recognise the emotions we are feeling and work through them is vital, rather than pushing them down, which we all know is very bad for our mental health and well-being and acts as a barrier between real and honest connections with others.

You can employ the thought process cycle mentioned above to recognise emotions and use the pause and reflect technique to work through these. In this way, we are taking control of our emotions rather than being controlled by them.

This technique can also be very useful in interactions with clients and difficult opponents on transactions. How are we reacting to them, and how might we react differently with a little pause that might be more beneficial to the relationship or the case? We will look at this in the Tools of Effectiveness Chapter in more detail.

Courage and Vulnerability

There is no doubt that being authentic requires courage. It also takes a willingness to be vulnerable. Vulnerability and lawyers aren't usually two words that you'd put together!

We're leaving the safety net of feeling that we fit in, of feeling that we're the same as our peer group or colleagues.

My first mentor shared this fantastic quote when we were training:

"Vulnerability can be our greatest strength.
When we stand in a place of being completely authentic, our true individual nature shines through and we become incomparable.
All the good stuff is on the other side of vulnerability."

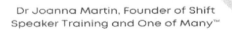

Dr Joanna Martin, Founder of Shift Speaker Training and One of Many™

I'm a commercial property lawyer. There are over 25,000 commercial property lawyers on the roll at the time of writing. How do I stand out amongst that crowd? How does one employment lawyer or corporate lawyer stand out?

Authenticity is our way of becoming incomparable, of connecting with our clients, peers, and people on the other side, which builds trust. That's why it's our Superpower!

But is Authenticity considered a weakness in law?

If authenticity involves emotional awareness and vulnerability, are these traits viewed with respect in our profession?

In my opinion, the first hurdle here is for you to come around to the idea that these are far from weaknesses. Let's return to self-awareness. You can't step into more authenticity if you're not aware of yourself and what's going on for you.

Hopefully, this book will start you thinking about your own opinion on vulnerability and authenticity and how you can use them in your life and career.

For me, it's not only not a weakness; it's a huge strength to step over the invisible line of being authentic and being vulnerable as a lawyer. We can step over that line and believe that this is what will set us apart; it's what will make us different, makes us more trustworthy to those we work with, better at networking, better at connecting with people on a real human level, where they like us as a person. You do business with those you know, like, and trust.

Being someone else is tiring and stressful. While taking steps toward becoming our authentic selves isn't easy, the more authentic we become, the easier everything becomes. In addition to turbocharging our networking, business development, team involvement, and leadership skills, increasing our authenticity improves our mental health and wellbeing, as we will discuss later on. When you see the results, there is no turning back again.

What Authenticity is not

Acting overconfidently

I love discussing the thorny issue of confidence with legal recruiters. I hear about candidates who act overconfidently in interviews because they think it's what they need to in order to appear right for the position. (Look back to the earlier points on character armour and what we have traditionally considered the archetypal lawyer to look and sound like). But, when they act overconfidently, that doesn't build trust or connection with their interviewers. Overconfidence is, in fact, the opposite of what we're talking about in this Chapter. It breaks down that trust and that connection.

Frequently people can see through it, and it's false. It's also rarely sustainable. If you achieve a position through overconfidence, imagine the energy and stress required to keep that going for the next 2, 3, or 5 years?

Dumping emotions all over everybody
I'm sure we've all worked in firms where the mood of the whole floor/team is dictated each day by the mood of the senior partner when they walk in. If they are in a bad mood, the whole floor/team is going to have a bad day. That is not what we want. Nobody wants to work in that sort of environment.

Authenticity is not about being so open with your emotions that you dump those emotions all over everyone else because you're having a bad day.

When we think about emotions and honesty in our workplace, we must use our judgement and common sense. You don't want everyone to know that you've had a fight with your other half before you came to work or that the children made you late for work because they wouldn't get ready for school. But on the other hand, if there's something challenging going on for you, it could be helpful for those who work closely with you to understand that something is hard for you at the moment.

A few years ago, I worked with a lovely junior partner client whose daughter underwent regular checkups following prior cancer treatment. Before each checkup, this partner was quite understandably preoccupied whilst waiting for the results of these checkups. The day before the appointment, she might be short-tempered and not the usual approachable open-door type of person.

By sharing the fact that the appointment was coming up, just as much as she was comfortable sharing, the juniors of the team didn't need to spend the day questioning what they had done wrong if they received a terse response to their question. And maybe the team would make their boss an extra cup of tea that day because they needed the support?

This boss is also role modelling the fact that it's okay to trust your team with the truth when you need a little more support. It's okay to say, "I'm not okay."

We need to use our judgment to bring the right level of honesty and emotion, which might not be an easy distinction. We do all have to use our common sense, but what I'd say is, don't be afraid of it.

As a role model, you're also showing others in the team that they can bring issues and concerns to you (or to their boss). This is going to be a vital component of effective leadership from now on.

Refusing to strive for what you want because you don't feel confident enough

My good friend and specialist legal recruiter Somaya Ouazzani and I often discuss the confidence gap in our respective clients' experiences. They might be perfect for a new role but don't feel they can take it. Their potential new firm has jumped at the chance to offer them a promotion and a higher salary and thinks they are perfect for the role, but the candidate can't see it.

Sometimes we do want something, but it's scary and outside our comfort zone, and then we talk ourselves out of it and say it's not the right thing for us.

But if we really want that thing, then that thing is for us.

Whether it's a promotion, whether it's a new role, whether it's asking if you can work four days a week because you want to run a pilates or a nutrition business on the fifth day, or become the manager of your eight year old's football team, whatever it is, it's about our identity, about who we really are and what we really want to do with our lives.

We need to find what we really want rather than accept the legal career conveyor belt on which we have found ourselves since we started out. Then finding a way to go after that thing, that's what authenticity is about.

It's easy to say, find out what you want and go after it. Not necessarily so easy to do. That's where a coach can be really useful. You will also find the exercises I've used on my journey (and regularly use with clients) in the Tools of Effectiveness Chapter coming up.

Being someone you're not

Authenticity is not about trying to be like everybody else. Although, in the short-term, emulating others might seem like the easier and safer route because we reduce the risk of rejection, in the longer term, trying to be someone else is tiring and damaging to our mental health and happiness. We also limit our potential drastically.

Finding a role model we really look up to is good to start. Don't try emulating someone who doesn't do things the way you'd like to or has created a life for themselves; that is the last thing you'd want. But, in the early few years finding someone you respect is a great starting point; just keep in mind those steps to take as you progress towards becoming more your authentic self.

It is becoming and being the person that you are capable of being that we are all capable of being.

That's where authenticity really is.

What could Authenticity look like for you?

Dropping the mask & the character armour

I'm afraid this won't happen the moment you finish reading this chapter or even the whole book. You won't wake up tomorrow and be your full authentic self. We would all be doing it if it was that easy, and I could charge a lot more for this book! It is steps on a journey. And I hope that this book and the tools and exercises I will share with you encourage you to think about how important it could be for you, identify some of the steps that you might like to take towards finding more of your authentic self, and the courage to live this, more and more each day.

It's learning to drop the character armour and the mask because, if nothing else, these are physically and metaphorically heavy to carry. It's hard trying to be someone you're not. It's stressful trying to be someone you're not. And it's not good for our career or our personal and professional development.

Being "present"

I know this has become something of a buzzword. Let me explain it in relation to a networking situation. Have you found yourself in a networking meeting listening to what the other person is saying and thinking, *"oh, I've got a really good point I'm going to make next*," or "oh, I must tell them about my experience with x, y, z client or transaction"?

You're busy thinking about what you're going to say in response to them. In doing that, you're not really being present with that person and not really listening to what they are saying. I would encourage you to give this a try next time, whether it's zoom or in-person networking, or even in a team meeting or when holding appraisals.

Let go of that ego voice that wants you to demonstrate your knowledge and experience instead of really listening. Give the other person the gift of your full attention because not many people will do that. That person will remember you as someone who really gave your time to listen to what they were saying.

You can use this in networking, appraisals with your team, and client pitches! Practice active listening, and show them that you're really listening. There might be a little bit of silence at the end when the other person finishes speaking; you haven't got your response prepared in your head because you were busy listening.

That's fine; let's not be afraid of the silence. They will remember your emotional openness, your lack of fear of silence, and appreciate the moment of genuine connection.

Another element to play with if you're networking is to avoid only discussing safe topics, the legal work you do, or the matters you've been dealing with recently. Instead, be brave enough to talk about important topics, things you care about and are interested in. Note: this is not talking about yourself but finding common ground topics you are both interested in.

"What's personal is universal."
Carl R. Rogers, On Becoming a Person: A Therapist's View of Psychotherapy

If you talk about something that's personal to you, you'll find a connection with the person you're networking with and can build stronger relationships.

Another networking tip here is to consider some topics you are genuinely interested in that can form the basis of some questions. I am genuinely interested in personal development, handling stress, and how the global pandemic has impacted people.

Easy questions for me (at the time of writing) include:

How much are you working from home since the pandemic?

How do you find it?

How has the pandemic impacted you, your business, and your family?

Find questions to get the other person talking about themselves, but on a topic, you can actively show your interest in it.

Braving emotion

Not being afraid of emotion. This is about not being afraid to share if we are having a difficult time and that we need some extra support. This means that ultimately, we have more connections with people, stronger and better, and more trusting connections with clients, peers, colleagues, and opponents, which will increase success in our career and certainly improve happiness and well-being.

It's not an easy journey to be more "*you.*" But once you've crossed that line, and you're saying to the world,

"*Yes, I am going to be more of who I am,*" then your sense of peace and wellbeing will increase because you're not trying to be somebody else.

The big question is, how can I be more authentic?

Just be yourself.

But of course, it's not that simple. If it were and everyone was doing it, it wouldn't be the Superpower I talk about!

Here are a few ideas for you to consider, and of course, the rest of the book and the resources on the website will build on these ideas.

1. Consider your vision and values. And doesn't that sound corporate? But no, this is about you.

2. What is your vision for your life? And this takes some thinking.

3. What do you want your life to look like?

4. And what are your values? What's important to you? What would we see running through you if we cut you in half down the middle (excuse the analogy)?

5. What are you? What is important to you?

6. Are you really living your life in accordance with your values?

7. Do you feel that you're in an organisation that supports you and your values?

8. What is your own version of success? The conveyor belt of the profession says this looks like: promotion, pay rise, buy a new house, buy new cars, etc. But what's your personal version of success?

Once I had ticked all those boxes, the title partner, great income, new house, new cars, I actually wasn't very happy. My version of success now is that I do work that I love, I bring in an income that supports the lifestyle we want, and I spend time with my family. If I have those three things, I feel successful. What does success feel like to you, to the authentic you?

And the bonus exercise. What was your six-year-old like? What did you love doing? We will consider these questions further in Chapters 4 and 5 with some fantastic exercises for you to try.

Authenticity is a key skill, something to be embraced by us and organisations for the mental health and happiness of all individuals and the efficiency and productivity of the business. It works to the advantage of the business and the people inside it, which is why it's so powerful!

"If you think dealing with issues like worthiness and authenticity and vulnerability are not worthwhile because there are more pressing issues, like the bottom line or attendance or standardized test scores, you are sadly, sadly mistaken. It underpins everything."

- Brene Brown.

Chapter 3
Character Traits of Lawyers

> **66**
>
> "Character is like a tree and reputation like a shadow. The shadow is what we think of it; the tree is the real thing."
>
> – ABRAHAM LINCOLN

Through my work with lawyers over the past few years, I've seen how certain character traits that tend to bring us into law negatively impact our mental health, stress levels, and general lack of happiness.

Here I want to talk a little about how impostor syndrome, perfectionism, and people-pleasing, relate specifically to lawyers. Or perhaps why this profession is uniquely placed on suffering from these character traits in larger proportions than in the general population.

Impostor Syndrome

"Impostor syndrome is a psychological pattern in which individuals doubt their skills, talents, or accomplishments and have a persistent internalised fear of being exposed as a "fraud." Despite external evidence of their competence, those experiencing this phenomenon remain convinced that they are frauds and do not deserve all they have achieved. Individuals with imposter syndrome incorrectly attribute their success to luck, or interpret it as a result of deceiving others into thinking they are more intelligent than they perceive themselves to be." (Wikipedia on Impostor syndrome)

It is a feeling that you're going to be caught out, found out as not being good enough, not really being qualified to do your job that you shouldn't really be there.

My husband went to a polytechnic rather than a red brick university and for many years felt that this meant he "shouldn't" be working in the same positions as colleagues from red brick establishments. I think some of this stigma may be lessening now, but I know it was a big help to him to discover one of his bosses and someone he respected was also from the same polytechnic! In the face of this "evidence" that if his colleague was "good enough" to be an equity partner, having come from the same educational background, so should he be. There is also comfort in feeling like others around you, which we will discuss further in this chapter.

Commonly believed to be an issue for predominately successful women, more recent research into imposter syndrome has found that it affects men and women equally. I certainly see it in both my male and female lawyer coaching clients.

The interesting point about impostor syndrome is that it doesn't diminish with age or experience as you might expect. Very experienced lawyers, including those in leadership positions, feel they aren't good enough or that they will somehow be discovered as a fraud.

Does this resonate with you?

Have you ever felt that you're not really worthy of your position, title, or salary? Or that you might lose it one day, be stripped of it, or be found out as not being what others expect you to be?

There are so many ways this might manifest itself.

For example:

- A lawyer might work far in excess of their contracted hours, always feeling that they haven't done enough; perhaps deep down, they feel they don't deserve a high salary, so they overwork to compensate, often without even realising it.

- Maybe you're a manager (a law firm owner even), and yet you can't quite leave the fee earning to your team; you need to keep your hand in just in case it all goes wrong, and you need to pay the mortgage with something! I've heard one client tell me he feels like he's earnt his money when he works on cases but not when he manages his team of over 50 lawyers!

- Perhaps you feel desperate for a new challenge on the one hand but the idea of not being an expert, being the newbie asking the questions, feels you with dread leaving you where you've been for years but gradually feeling worse and worse about it.

Here are a few strategies that you might like to use to counteract these feelings:

1. Impostor syndrome can spring from a lack of inner confidence (refer to the Confidence Chapter). Working on increasing your inner confidence will help to manage some of those feelings of an imposter when they pop up.
2. Talk about it. Feeling that we are similar to others helps us to manage some of the emotions that come when we feel we are different somehow.

   "A problem shared is a problem halved" works here. If we accept that 74-83% of lawyers suffer from impostor syndrome, would it make us feel any better when we notice it rearing its head in our careers? (https://www.lawyer-monthly.com/2020/05/impostor-syndrome-and-how-it-impacts-your-career-success/)

3. Keep a record of your wins, excellent feedback or testimonials, letters, or gifts from grateful clients. These "evidences" disagree with your inner impostor voice. I recommend clients keep a "brag jar" or email folder. You don't have to label it in a brag folder; it could be testimonials or feedback. Keep your excellent testimonials, award wins, and mentions from clients or partners in your team in this folder.

This is your evidence folder that you are certainly not an impostor and are in fact the exceptional lawyer I know you are! If someone gives you a compliment personally or on your work, make sure you keep a record.

If you receive a thank you card or a gift, take a photo and save it in your email evidence folder. If a client calls you and says what an amazing job you've done, email yourself a note of what they've said and save it to your email folder. Perhaps ask them if you can use their comments as a testimonial.

This evidence folder is useful for performance reviews, promotions, pay rises, and marketing, but even more importantly, you can dip into it if you're having a low day or need a bit of a boost. It will provide you with the evidence your mind needs to counteract that impostor feeling.

Perfectionism

"Perfectionistic tendencies have been linked to a laundry list of clinical issues: depression and anxiety (even in children), obsessive-compulsive disorder, binge eating, and other eating disorders, post-traumatic stress disorder, chronic fatigue syndrome, insomnia, chronic headaches, and, even early mortality and suicide." (https://www.bbc.com/future/article/20180219-toxic-perfectionism-is-on-the-rise)

Perfectionism is an interesting one, isn't it? Who wouldn't want to be a perfectionist lawyer on the face of it? All of that attention to detail, always striving to be the best, to create the most elegantly drafted and all situation encompassing clauses, drafting the best legal arguments, and always being a step ahead of the other side?

Great!

Someone who gets everything absolutely spot on 100% of the time in real life. But that character isn't a real human being, or at least not for the vast majority of us. This is fiction. However, it is a fiction many in our profession are still trying to emulate every day.

A 26-year-old qualified commercial lawyer once expressed frustration that no matter how many years of experience, he still felt like he was missing important points and was waiting to get tripped up. I could hear that he was expecting himself to be able to craft the perfect contracts with no loopholes, no downsides for his clients, nothing they could remotely criticise him for. It seemed this was a stage he had expected to reach in his career after 26 years. I very much doubt that this lawyer is on his own in his thinking and his high and perhaps unrealistic expectations of himself.

Perfectionists tend to set unrealistically high expectations of themselves, are quick to find faults within themselves, and are overly critical of their own mistakes.

They might find that they spend a lot of time procrastinating over decisions. These decisions might be as simple as giving a final draft document the sign-off for completion or even deciding whether to go for a promotion or a new role.

Perfectionists often look to specific individuals, whether it be their boss or their client, for validation or approval. They don't tend to look into themselves for that validation that they are doing a great job. If you're looking for that validation and praise from a client and something goes awry in that relationship, the pain of losing that approval and feelings of failure, are all the worse and can result in a big fall in confidence. Perfectionists also shy away from compliments and don't stop to recognise their successes; however big or small, they are immediately on to the next thing.

In an ideal world, a lawyer would look inside themselves and know that they are good enough without constant external validation. I hope this book goes some way to helping you to do just that.

If we see perfectionism as a good and useful trait in a lawyer, as I suspect many past hiring managers would, what's the problem?

I've already highlighted a tendency towards procrastination, which can be harmful to transactions, billing, time recording, and relationships if taken too far. On the simplest level (and perhaps the most immediate concern for a law firm) is the impact on time recording and, as a consequence, billing. It's so common for lawyers to "sense check" their time before recording it to the file. They waste valuable time in the day constantly assessing how much time is "reasonable" to put on the matter and how much faster Joe Bloggs might have completed that task. Not only is that valuable brainpower wasted, but frequently they go on to record far less time than they have actually spent. In some studies, about half!

Imagine those "losses" the firms are taking, which they could prevent with some support and training for their lawyers.

On an individual level, it can result in the lawyer avoiding challenges such as a new position or role or taking on more responsibility. It can produce a lack of creativity and imaginative thinking, which can be very useful when we're problem-solving for clients. Feelings of failure, low self-esteem, and low confidence are common, even leading to anxiety, depression, and OCD.

What can be done to stop perfectionism from being a hindrance to success & achievement?

There may be two angles to approach this from. Firstly, at the firm or organisational level and at the individual level.

Traditionally firms have recruited for traits like perfectionism, probably known as attention to detail, people-pleasing, always saying yes, and being willing to go the extra mile. These would be seen as conducive traits to being a great lawyer.

It would be refreshing for hiring managers to see that whilst in the short term these might produce more profit, in the longer term, you may face stagnation in that person's career as they begin to feel more and more powerless and afraid to step outside of their comfort zone.

The sense of creativity in their work, business development skills, personal growth, self-confidence, and self-esteem, begin to be more and more negatively impacted.

Much like impostor syndrome, perfectionism does not decrease with time and experience as you might expect. It is likely to become more prominent and potentially debilitating as time goes on. There is also a possible mental health cost in terms of absence through stress or the opting out by the lawyer who decides that a challenging role isn't for them, resulting in the organisation facing replacement, recruitment, and retraining costs. If, instead of looking for "attention to detail," aka perfectionism, hiring practices emphasized having a growth mindset, creativity, and a willingness to explore outside our comfort zones, these traits might be recognised as more desirable.

Our firms' ongoing culture and training have a great role to play outside of hiring. Again a culture of encouraging a growth mindset, trying new things, and expanding beyond the safety of our comfort zones, with the backing and support of the firm, should be welcomed.

Mistakes are perhaps one of the greatest fears of all lawyers. There are firms where people are terrified to admit a potential mistake, or when following a mistake, they have felt side-lined, pushed out, found themselves unable to remain at the firm, or took extended sick leave due to the stress. How a firm approaches this topic can define whether a lawyer lives in constant fear with all the negatives that come with this or whether they feel supported and safe to do their best without a fixation on something going wrong. Alternatively, some organisations encourage openness from day one. As part of their induction meetings, new recruits hear about mistakes senior partners have made, showing new staff that it is not the career-ending disaster we might have been made to believe in the past. Some say you aren't a real lawyer until you've dealt with a claim.

That sense of understanding that it can and does happen, and it's not the end of a career or even the loss of respect or reputation that we all fear, encourages people to discuss these things more openly. Lawyers are only human, after all.

For us to see that perfectionist tendency, far from being an asset, needs to be managed to support mental health, growth, achievement, and that feeling of psychological safety in our role would be a great step forward.

As to you as an individual, what steps could you take to limit the negative impacts of a perfectionist mentality on your career and sense of job satisfaction?

My clients often hear from me that realisation is half the battle. Even without coaching, therapy, or any exploration beyond realising something is an issue for you; you will be able to make tweaks and changes. What we don't know about, we can't change.

If on reading this chapter, you think that some of my comments on perfectionism, impostor syndrome, or people pleaser might relate to you, I urge you to take notice of that realisation. Perhaps start to get curious about it. Explore where you see it popping up and in what situations, what events or comments tend to trigger those feelings?

Is it just at work or at home as well? Is it with your supervisor/your boss, or clients, peers, or opponents on the other side?

Case study:

Gemma is a self-employed lawyer who came to work with me as she started her consultancy business. She confessed to feeling her inner imposter syndrome rear its head when her opponent had a "posh" accent. Being from the north with a strong accent herself, she felt "less than" or "judged."

Just by naming this feeling and discussing it with a third party, it began to feel "less," and I haven't heard her mention this feeling for a few years, and business is booming for her!

When we experience repeating thoughts that aren't good for us, it's useful to ask ourselves if those thoughts are really true. Or whether they are just a pattern of thoughts that have become well established over years of repetition but are not, in fact, the truth. I suggest that clients carry a notebook or their phone and jot down a note of the thoughts that come up and in what situations. What triggered or caused those thoughts to come up? A pattern might emerge about what sort of situations generally give rise to those not so useful feelings. Once we can see a pattern, it might be something we can interrupt, break and replace with an alternative way of thinking. Over time those repetitive thoughts of needing to be "perfect" and not put a foot wrong can be replaced by something more positive, helpful, and empowering.

The brag jar idea I mentioned in relation to impostor syndrome is relevant here as well.

There is a general acceptance of the idea that for every negative, it takes 6 or 7 positives to counteract it (perhaps even more for lawyers than the general population?), so if we have seven pieces of positive feedback and one negative, that negative is all we will focus on. Keeping a record of all the good feedback, testimonials, gifts from clients, and thanks from your opponent, are all things you can draw upon when you might be tempted to fixate on one negative comment.

Group or peer support, and understanding just how common this trait is, can also be extremely helpful. Like so many feelings, realising that you are not alone and that quite a few others actually feel very similar to you helps to normalise the feelings. It takes away some of the sense of feeling that you're not as good as others and that you're alone in having these thoughts or feelings.

Where once upon a time the legal profession was felt to be very closed and secretive, where people from separate firms rarely socialised, perhaps for fear of sharing trade secrets(!) now, there are many groups, events, and initiatives where people can come together and share their experiences. Or simply to talk about something non-work-related with people who "get it."

I'd encourage everyone reading this book to find a group or network you can get involved with, whether inside your firm, your particular sector, or something more general. You'll be improving your networking skills at the same time and might even make some great future connections. I will include great networking groups on the resources section of the website as I come across these. And, don't be afraid to organise your own!

People Pleaser

The final character trait I'd like to mention here is a people pleaser. If you told the outside world that lawyers were generally people-pleasers, they would find that amusing.
In your own experience, looking around at the people you work with when a client says jump, do they ask "how high"?

What exactly is a people pleaser?

These are people who never want to say no; they want to do everything right and fear disappointing others, whether they are clients, peers, or their firm management. With more junior lawyers, a strong people pleaser can look like constant check-ins, frequently doubting their own work, and requiring constant reassurance. In senior lawyers, it might manifest as a need to look after or please their clients in a way that potentially damages their personal and work relationships as well as their health.

I once worked with an experienced rainmaking partner who would frequently be at his client's offices at 7:00 am to collect documents whenever they called. I also remember some of his clients refusing to pay for a job at the agreed point, saying they would only pay six months later (and then disappearing on a £100k+ holiday to the Caribbean). Many of us on the team refuse to work for them again!

So why do we do it?

The people-pleaser trait is rooted in fear. Fear of rejection, isolation, or abandonment. It is frequently a product of the character trait that brings us into law, combined with us than being trained by those who simply replicate the trait into their trainees/juniors and also by firms who historically have hired and rewarded for such traits.

It might be a fear of losing the client, of loss of revenue, maybe loss of reputation. I certainly fell into that trap in the early years of my own legal business. I was so busy client pleasing that I would work until 10 pm most days, have unnecessary telecons late into the night and felt that my clients completely controlled my life. I still can't listen to a Nokia ring tone!

I've learnt perhaps the hard way that it's important to know when I have to, or even when I want to, say "no" without fear. This behaviour was rooted in having a scarcity mentality that there would never be enough work or enough clients. Since recognising this scarcity fear, I can be more selective about the clients I work with and aim to take on mainly polite clients who pay their bills!

Some may say that you need to be adaptable in the early part of building a career or a business (whether that's your own business or your practice inside your firm), and I have some sympathy with that. For a year or two, you might have to work with clients who are not ideal, but the goal of getting to a position where you can be more choosy should always be kept in mind. A destination where you can say "no" to the wrong things for you.

It's about realising and remembering your worth as a lawyer and as a person. I hope this book will stand you in good stead on this journey.

Chapter 4.

Tools of Effectiveness

66

"Your time is limited, so don't waste
it living someone else's life.
Don't let the noise of others' opinions
drown out your own inner voice. And
most important, have the courage to
follow your heart and intuition.
They somehow already know what
you truly want to become.
Everything else is secondary."

- STEVE JOBS

Let's think about machines as opposed to human beings for a moment…

We completely understand the importance of parts and mechanisms to be maintained and serviced. We service our cars every year (or as regularly as the manufacturer recommends). We use the right fuel for our petrol or diesel engines, and we fill the tank up before it's running on empty because that would cause damage to the engine and it would be expensive to repair.

We don't take the same care of ourselves.

The time for money model that we lawyers work inside was created in the industrial revolution era. I would suggest that it is not so ridiculous to compare humans to machines, especially where our business and working model is already predicated on the basis that we work like machines. If you want more output, increase the hours worked. Is it little wonder that firms who want to make larger profits simply increase the target of chargeable hours? It's cheaper than hiring more people. But even machines tire and become less effective if they're left constantly running without proper care and maintenance.

A senior lawyer once told me her firm's management team openly admitted that law firms are so profitable because lawyers aren't paid overtime...

Humans, unlike machines, have a few extra needs in order to work effectively. If you want to increase your personal effectiveness, please consider some of these points and try some of the exercises I've suggested in this chapter. If you also manage people, you can use some of the tips and tools in this Chapter to help your team be more effective.

I'd like to caveat that I don't use the term effective, to imply that I'm only interested in the output. Again another throwback to the industrial era. If you haven't picked up by now, I'm actually really interested in improving our profession's health, well-being, and happiness. But firms are businesses with bottom lines, so I'm appealing to the desire to improve performance in my request that people take better (or, in fact, any) care of themselves.

It isn't just the organisation; it's also the individual. Several interesting comments arose in my research into why lawyers don't delegate. Individuals felt the need to be "in control" to be "the best."

I'm attempting to mobilise those inherent overachiever and perfectionist tendencies to persuade you around to my way of thinking. I hope it's working!

If you take better care of your basic needs, you will be more efficient, productive, and profitable. Is that enough of a reason to persuade you to try it?

Basic needs

If we identify our basic needs and work on ensuring that these are met, we get ourselves to the lofty heights of feeling "okay." Not amazing, not on fire, not feeling like we can take on anything, just "okay." But okay is a good starting place, and for some, it's a higher level of care for themselves than they've allowed before now!

From "okay," we can handle the day-to-day with more ease and have a little more in the reserve tank to cope with anything additional that is thrown at us or if we need to help someone else. It's easy to think of life and work as separate entities, and some people would advocate that it's healthier to think of them as separate. While I would agree that we should have boundaries and distinctions and work on improving these, I don't agree that we can stop one flowing over into the other as humans.

We might be in a great place at work where all is going well for us. Our clients and team love us, and we're meeting or even exceeding our targets. I wonder how long we could carry on like that if we have issues at home, perhaps with our relationship or the health of a loved one, perhaps even an injury making life harder for us.

Similarly, if everything is going well at home and you have great relationships with your significant other and children, but then something happens at work - that equally leaks over into your sense of well-being at home. It's from this perspective I believe that taking good care of our needs and, therefore, our well-being benefits us both at work and at home.

Let's take a closer look at needs. I've recorded a more in-depth video training on my website resources section, but I'm going to try and explain the same idea here.

I've already suggested that if we take care of our basic needs, we get to the enviable position of "okay." If we don't look after our basic needs, we feel ill, not ourselves, off-kilter, not quite right, etc. Looking at basic needs is often a starting point for me with clients who are on the verge of burnout or depression.

If you can find the energy to focus on your basic needs, it will support you through the hard times and into better ones. It builds resilience.

As humans (as living beings even), we have certain needs that we share in common. Food, water, shelter, and sleep would be on everyone's list. After that, it becomes a little more personalised. You might need to give this part a little thought or even explore the idea for a week or two. What else do you need in order to feel okay? That without it, you would feel unwell or off-kilter?

For me, the additional needs include meditation which started as a nice to have but is now a complete necessity for me if I'm going to stay on course, stay motivated and keep out that pesky imposter syndrome. I also know that meditation was my replacement for antidepressants, and I'm not foolish enough to believe that without following my daily practice, I won't sooner or later slip back into stress-induced thinking and lose some of my perspective and positivity.

In fact, when the global pandemic started and my stress levels rose again to the "waking in the night" levels, increasing my meditation each day kept me going.

The final basic need I have is - time alone. This was a fairly recent realisation for me. I thrive on a bit of quiet time with a book, a podcast, a notepad, or a laptop. I didn't know it was a need until my youngest son was born, and he was about four months old. I woke up one Saturday in a terrible mood, I felt out of sorts, I was angry with everyone. After a bit of thought, I realised it had been months since I last had any time to myself. I'd been with Vic day and night, and as much as I love my kids, I can't spend all my time in anyone's company. I need a bit of time out, even if it's an hour a week when there's no one else around me. This was one of my biggest struggles in lockdown!

So my basic needs are food, sleep, water, shelter, meditation, and time alone.

What are your basic needs? On the resources section of the website, you can download a Needs Chart for you to complete and keep on your wall. You can tell your other half or older children what it is. They might want their own list or chart on the wall. If you get to the end of the week and feel grouchy or out of sorts, have a look at your chart and see if your basic needs have been met that week. If not, how can you replenish these in the following week?

Some of my clients share their charts with the family and have older children saying, "you're in a bad mood today; where are you up to on your chart?" - maybe we'll have office ones one day?!

In my needs training video, you'll see that I go on to talk about the differences between Needs and Wants. Wants are things like chocolate, chips, and alcohol (yes, they aren't basic needs, I'm afraid). When we are full up and our basic needs are taken care of, adding a few wants enhance our experience, and we feel enjoyment. Having our needs not met means that we try to up with wants instead, which creates bad habits and even addictions and dependencies.

I'll give you this challenge. The next time you reach the end of the week and are counting the hours until you can have that glass of wine, gin, and tonic, or bottle of beer, ask yourself first if you've had enough water that day, had enough sleep that week and eaten since breakfast. If yes, go ahead and enjoy that drink. If you arrive home exhausted, starving, and having not had any fluids since your 11 am coffee, maybe it's time to think twice.

As with many things, it's about balance. The ebb and flow of balance, not rigid scales. One week you might have a trial or a big completion. You may work late and eat poorly. You can't change a lot at that moment, but the realisation is more than half the battle. Realise that you need to prioritize getting more rest and eating better the next week. And, don't beat yourself up.

Sleep

If meeting your basic needs is something you decide to prioritize (and I hope it is), you will find you can function more effectively, achieve more, have more energy, and have a more positive mindset.

Although I encourage you to identify your own personal needs, it would be a mistake not to highlight sleep in particular. There is emerging research that sleep is so important to our health that a severe lack of sleep might be more detrimental to our health than smoking.

When my dad was diagnosed with prostate cancer, his lack of effective sleep was considered a risk factor for surgery, and radiotherapy was opted for instead.

Fortunately, this proved successful, but it was the first time I had understood how important a lack of sleep could be to our organs and our general body health.

Non-lawyers often ask me just how effective and accurate we can really be by 3 am on the second night of a large completion. That is to say nothing of the impact we know sleep deprivation has on our mental faculties. I know as well as the next lawyer what a badge of honour it can be to be the last person standing at a completion meeting at 3 am.

Would you complete one of these deals and be in the final negotiations at the end while under the influence of alcohol? No? Well, sleeping less than 3 to 4 hours for more than three nights is the equivalent of a .10 blood alcohol.

If you needed heart surgery, would you want the surgeon who had been working since 8 am operating on you or even reviewing your medical notes and making decisions at 11 pm or later?!

So how do we get more sleep and more quality sleep?

Here are some tips:

1. No screens before bed. Test this for yourself. Try having no screens for half an hour and if there is no

improvement, try for an hour before bed. The blue light interferes with your serotonin levels and affects your natural sleep patterns. This applies to your kids as well.

2. Turn off the Wi-Fi due to the Electromagnetic Field radiation adversely impacting sleep cycles.

3. Go to sleep at the same time and wake at the same time each day, even on weekends.

4. Develop a gratitude practice. Think of three things to be grateful for that day before you go to sleep. Studies conducted by the Heart Math Institute prove the benefit of this simple practice to our hearts and our sleep! (You can find a mini-training on gratitude practices on the website).

5. Adopt a common bedtime routine, including gratitude or meditation, to help control the early morning waking, procrastination, and ruminating, which I refer to in the resources on the website.

6. No caffeine after 2 pm. It may be earlier or later for you, but this was my rule until I stopped having

caffeinated coffee (which incidentally gives me much more energy at the end of the day, and I sleep better!). Test it out for yourself.

While writing this section on sleep, I know how important it is - but I appreciate that for many lawyers reading this book, it will seem like a pipe dream to be able to get more sleep.

I've added a suggested list of further research in the website resources section. Perhaps instead of asking how to find more time for sleep, you could pick one of these tips (or any you prefer from a number of much better-qualified professionals than me) and put this into practice initially. It's about small baby steps towards your goal.

And don't forget: Effective = Profitable

Values

A popular topic in the coaching world is the idea of living life in accordance with your values. Life is harder than it needs to be if we aren't living in accordance with our personal values. It's also often harder for us to make decisions if we don't use our values as a guide or as a lens through which we see the world.

But what does it mean to live life in accordance with your values? And what exactly are your values? You may have done a similar exercise before and already be clear on your life values. If this was fairly recent and you're happy that they remain the same, there is no need to repeat this part of the exercise. If you've never considered what your personal life values are, or you haven't for some time, I encourage you to work through this one with me.

Terms like "vision" and "values" can feel a little artificial as we've probably all worked in firms or organisations that have corporate values, mission statements, and visions, which may or may not actually be true. This may have been for the benefit of outside parties and clients rather than being true to the culture of the firm or organisation. I therefore encourage you to leave any preconceptions about the term "values" behind. We are looking at your personal, individual, and true values.

Leave anyone else, like your other half, kids, clients, or boss, at the door for this exercise. This exercise is just about you. Later, you could repeat this with your other half and even older children and develop a set of family values. Or even with your immediate team and create team values.

First, it's important to identify your own, as they are your main driving force and the lens through which you see the world and make your decisions.

On the website's resources section, you will find a specimen list of values. This isn't an exhaustive list, and you should feel free to come up with your own words. The important thing is what that word means to you rather than how others might define it. For example, in my mind, I think several values like charity, contribution, and giving back might be summed up as contributions. You can decide which words work best for you by looking at that list of specimen values or the brief list I've included in the exercise box below. Which of these words feel important to you in relation to the way you live your life?

Resist the temptation to choose lots of them. They all sound like great values, but which five are most important to you?

Put another way, if you could only live your life in accordance with 5 of them, which would they be?

I say only five as if you try to live life in accordance with 7 or 10 or 15 values; you will very likely find that hard to achieve. 5 is a more manageable number.

If you're wondering if a certain thing is of value or not, ask yourself whether you could put it into a wheelbarrow. So books or money would not be a value, but education, learning or wealth, or abundance would be a value.

My top value has always been freedom. I believed that this was because I was self-employed, but I realise it goes deeper than that. I took more GCSEs and A-levels, and I needed to keep as many options open as possible in every step. I like having choices or feeling as though I have choices. I've also realised that I want my children and my clients to feel that they have choices too and to feel confident enough (see inner confidence in Chapter 1) to make the right choices and decisions for their lives. Enabling them to find the right path for them whatever that is - that is freedom to me.

How does understanding my top value impact my life and business? How can this knowledge help us? At the time I did the values exercise first time around, I'd been self-employed for about three years. But it was, at that point, that I was working 12 to 14-hour days very regularly. For quite a time, I convinced myself that it was still freedom because I was at home, and I was able to see my children - as they ate tea and watched television even though I was behind a laptop and constantly asking them to be quiet as I made yet another conference call. The trap of success in any role is that the reward for hard work is more hard work. The more successful my business was, the harder I was working.

At a retreat in 2016, I discovered that a) freedom was my top and guiding value, and b) I wasn't living that value because the hours I was working meant that I did not feel free at all. In fact, I felt trapped by my own business. This realisation was the catalyst for introducing many changes. I learnt to delegate, build a team around me, and worry less about handing overwork and client relationships to others. I also learnt to start valuing my time more and be more selective about what I said yes and no to, just to be more aware. The shift in less than six months was amazing.

My business produced the same income, but I had drastically reduced the amount of time I spent on my laptop, managed to get away from the phone, and even had a two-week holiday - when I didn't work!

Now, when I start to feel stuck or overwhelmed, a good starting point is to see where my value boundaries are being overstepped. Of course, like any situation of balance, there are ebbs and flows. Sometimes I work long hours or when I'm on holiday, but it remains the exception rather than the rule and only when I've made a conscious decision to do it. Remember, if you've been doing something for more than three months, it's your new normal, and you should make decisions from that place rather than waiting for it to change on its own.

If you're faced with a decision, it's often helpful to put it through the lens of your top values to help you decide what might be the best path for you to choose. As you become more familiar with your top values, making decisions this way is likely to become more and more unconscious.

One of my favourite questions about values is what happens if my other half and I have different values, even conflicting ones. I think the same questions could easily apply to a team or someone you tend to work side-by-side with at work, or even a business partner.

The answer is not that you're not matched, and your relationship is doomed. But quite the opposite.

Understanding and appreciating others' values will help you see why they make their decisions. It might be completely opposite to the way you would make the decision, or they appear to have their priorities completely different from yours. By understanding their motivation for these decisions, you can have different and more useful conversations about how you can best support each other.

My husband and I experience this quite regularly as my top value of freedom butts right up against his top value of stability and security! But at least we understand where each other is coming from. When I want to invest in the business, rather than risking our future and suffering sleepless nights, we work out how to do what I want to do whilst minimising the risks.

You can find more resources to help you identify your values on my website, and if you manage a team, I'd highly recommend you try the exercise as a group.

Changing Your Language

The language we choose can keep us stuck. The words we use both internally to ourselves and externally to the outside world affect the way we feel. If we say to ourselves inwardly or out loud to others that we are busy or stressed, we will continue to feel busy and stressed.

Being busy is a badge of honour for lawyers - a busy lawyer must be a good lawyer - they must be valuable and in demand. Of course, we all want to believe we are valuable; the key is to find that inner feeling of being of value without also needing to feel busy.

In my case, I came to a combination of realisations. Firstly as mentioned in Chapter 5, re-delegating, I started to think about my notional hourly rate and about the activities I was spending my time on. If someone else could do those activities cheaper than me, this would free up more of my time to do the activities only I could do (e.g., client meetings, networking, writing this book, or training to be a coach).

Sometimes it might be skipping after-school club and taking ice creams to the park on a sunny day. By thinking about my time in monetary terms, I was able to start being more strict about what I was spending my time doing. By delegating, I was also creating jobs and work for other people.

The second shift for me was to start thinking about what success really meant to me. What success really means is a common theme throughout this book, and if you take nothing else away from it, please give a thought as to what your own personal version of success looks like. When I realised that success for me meant having time to enjoy my life, to do the things I wanted to do without feeling busy and stressed, I felt able to let go of the need to validate myself by being "busy."

Who would we really consider more successful? The person who works 12-14 hour days or someone who works as few hours as possible for the same or more reward and enjoys their work? In my opinion, it's certainly no measure of success to work 12-hour days; in fact, it's the contrary. To have the income and lifestyle I want to have, work around my family, and enjoy what I do is my definition of success.

It wasn't always like this; I was that parent who was "busy" every day at the school gates as I dropped off my eldest son and dashed for a train. I think it's why I don't feel all that connected to the mums at school - as every time they asked how I was; I would reply that I was so busy and I was always running late. It's no wonder they stopped asking how I was - that sort of energy radiates from people, and no one else wants to catch it!

I challenge you to become more aware of your everyday language. What is slipping out of your mouth so unconsciously, so automatically that you don't register it? Notice it. Other lawyers probably already have it and so possibly don't even notice. Notice how it leaves you feeling and also how it leaves those around you feeling. In an office environment, of course, it multiplies and becomes even more important to address the culture of the workplace.

There are other language patterns we need to be vigilant for. I'm going into coach mode now - a common belief is that "I'm not good enough." This emerges in many forms, the need for perfectionism, fearing the judgement of others, including peers, clients, or the boss, if we fail to meet that perfect or impossible standard. The feeling that we're not as good, experienced, quick, detailed, personable, and ambitious [insert your word here] as our peer Joe Bloggs is another form of I'm not good enough.

We are not the same as human beings or as lawyers, but for years, firms have played the comparison game encouraging employees to reach higher billing or utilization targets because Jo Bloggs sitting next to you is doing it. I believe these days of the unnecessarily competitive, damaging, and demotivating practices are over or certainly, I hope, on their way out.

Why do we set employees against each other instead of creating strong, stable, supportive, and productive teams? Good relationships at work impact happiness, well-being, effectiveness, productivity, and profit.

You get the idea - addressing the "*I'm not good enough*" voice in our heads (however that manifests for you) will help you to overcome many obstacles on the way to creating more content, happy, and successful life (whatever that means to you).

Other forms "I'm not good enough" might take include: not feeling ready for a promotion or a new position even though everyone else thinks you'd be the perfect fit for it, feeling intimidated by a salary or a package on offer, or feeling underqualified or not worthy of what's on offer.

Tips for dealing with the "I'm not good enough" or "I'm not worthy" voice:

1. Invest in yourself by taking on a coach or mentor or taking some personal development courses. Even by taking that step and making that investment in yourself and your growth, you are sending a message to yourself (and to the universe if you like) that you are worth it.

2. Try daily affirmations or positive statements repeated each day or written down and placed somewhere you will see them regularly, like on your desk or near the kettle.

3. Meditation. I know I sound like a broken record when it comes to this, but it helps to improve confidence and self-esteem and certainly does absolutely no harm to your mental health!

4. Consider your needs using the exercises referred to in this Chapter. Taking care of "you" increases your sense of being worth taking care of and is a great first step to increasing self-worth and self-esteem.

Chapter 5.

Goals, Vision & Direction

"In the absence of clearly defined goals, we becoming strangely loyal to performing daily acts of trivia."

‒ UNKNOWN

This quote really spoke to me when thinking about my career in law and probably even more so since I became a parent. I lived as I see so many people do, getting through the day (8.30 am to 4.30 pm was my return to work day), rushing home in the traffic, blood pressure rising, reaching nursery at 6 pm on the dot to collect the last baby there - my gorgeous Teddy, (the designer of this book cover!)

I remember getting him into the car and checking my blackberry to see how the corporate transaction I was working on was going.

I'd get Teddy home, fed, and into bed before logging back on. And so each day went. If you'd asked me what my goals were, it would have been to get through each day and to try and be a decent mum. I didn't see anything beyond what I was doing each day, and I'd have no more energy for anything else. I was on the conveyor belt.

My journey into entrepreneurship began during my maternity leave in 2010/2011, and I loved it - although my first business attempt (online organic children's clothing) was a bit of a money pit and not much else. It did show me how much I enjoyed working and doing business. I quickly realised that I could make more money in law, and fortunately, I met the founder of one of the first fee share law firms, and the rest, as they say, is history.

Even in building my new legal business, I didn't have goals. I didn't stop to think about what the big picture was. What the aim of my life was. Or what my 3, 5, or 10-year plan looked like. Again it was survival every day and trying to be a good mum. You notice the common theme.

In March 2016, I sat down to decide what I really wanted.

What did I want my life to look like? What did I want to achieve in the next 5 to 7 years? I wanted to learn about money and investing so that I could create a future with my husband where we had choices.

I thank Ann Wilson (the Wealth Chef) for my early education in managing finances and wealth and learning to invest in myself. Since my LPC, I hadn't invested in my own growth, and most of that was funded by my first firm! I learnt how to calculate how much money we actually needed for the life we wanted. Then I had a goal!

I also thought hard about what I did and didn't want from my career. I know it was easier for me in many ways to make changes by being self-employed. I am in charge of my diary to a very large degree. But I work with many employed clients and tell them it's not usually about quitting a job (sometimes it is, but not as often as you'd think). It's about remembering who you are, the authenticity piece, and what you love.

Incorporating more of what you want into your life. Some of my clients take up dancing lessons, art, or play more golf.

What are your personal and financial goals? Think 3, 5, or 10 years ahead. I've included a goalsetting worksheet in the resources section of my website.

Check-in regularly with your goals. How are you doing? Do you need to adjust them?

My mentor gave me a great piece of advice: If you've been doing something for more than three months, it's your new normal.

What do I mean by that? Don't put your goals or goalsetting on hold indefinitely in relation to goals. It can be very tempting to think things like; I'm in a really busy period at work at the moment, my parents are ill, the baby doesn't sleep, etc. In some cases, that situation is truly temporary.

In many cases, that situation isn't going to change any time soon, if at all. You shouldn't put your goals, dreams, or life on hold for too long.

If, as you read this, you're thinking I would like to do X, and I'll do it when Y happens. Ask yourself if that situation has existed for more than three months. If it has, I encourage you to accept that Y isn't happening and plan from that place instead.

Goals are amazingly powerful. They focus the mind on identifying what we actually want or don't want in our lives. Writing down your goals means you're 42% more likely to achieve them - so try using my resource sheet.

Getting accountable to someone about your goals makes you 85 to 95% more likely to achieve them. That's crazy. We are often happy to let ourselves down, but we don't like letting others down. Especially lawyers. We are hardwired to deliver what we say we will deliver. You can use that particularly annoying trait to your advantage. Get brave, reach out and find someone to get accountable to. It could be your partner at home or a friend or colleague.

I have a regular call with my accountability buddy. We know each other's businesses and what our respective business priorities are. We share what we aim to get done before we next speak, and we don't like letting the other person down, so we usually get done what we say we'll get done; we've even started a property investment business together!

You might decide to set daily or weekly goals about whatever needs prioritising at that time. Getting these important things completed and off your mental to-do list frees you up to having more mental energy for other things. Constantly procrastinating over the task we really don't want to do, takes up so much energy to just keep putting it off.

To reach your goals, you might need to have a more effective handle on your use of time and energy, and we cover suggestions for this in the Tools of Effectiveness Chapter.

You might also benefit from delegating appropriate tasks elsewhere. This might be a delegation at work, or perhaps it's getting a cleaner, using online food shopping and delivery, getting a gardener, or sending shirts to the dry cleaners for washing and ironing? For £10 a week, this is something my husband wishes he had done years ago!

Something I found a huge help in learning to delegate (and accept help) was using the outdated legal model in my favour. If my charge out rate is £250 or £350 an hour (insert yours), even if it's £75-£100 an hour, does it make sense for me to be washing and ironing at that rate when someone else can do it at a fraction of the cost? Realising this has given me permission to take on and make the most of having a PA, a legal secretary, and support staff when needed them. I really recommend we start thinking like a business even if we are an individual lawyer employed in a traditional firm. Your time is valuable – what are you doing with it, and is it helping you to achieve your goals or holding you back?

You can find a number of exercises to help you identify your goals on my website under the resources section, including a recording to talk you through the "ideal day" exercise and a goals worksheet.

For now, you could try simply closing your eyes for a few moments and thinking about your future. Try asking yourself what you'd like to see around you, what are you spending your time doing, and who with? What does your life look like in 3 months, 12 months, three years, five years, and ten years time?

Vision

What is your vision for your life, for your future?

I wonder if you've ever stopped to think about it over the last 5 or 10 years?

From the age of 13 years old, all I wanted to do was become a solicitor. But from that early age, I was determined that I wanted a desk, a computer, and a briefcase, although now I carry a bright purple backpack! My high school teachers told I could be anything I wanted to be as I had good grades, including a doctor or a politician! I remember my Grandma was very disappointed in me. When my teenage self told her what I wanted to do, she replied (as a farmer), "couldn't you do something useful, like be a vet"!

Aside from my "dream" of becoming a lawyer, I didn't think any further into my future. As I got older, my "vision" became having a good job, buying a house, and starting a family when I met my now-husband. By the age of 35 years old, I had all of these things and no real idea of where to go next. We do need something to get up for in the morning. I had my children and family, of course, and by that stage, a successful legal business, but for many of us "high" or even "over" achievers, we need to be doing something we feel is worthwhile, perhaps a challenge even. Somewhere along the way, starting running my business became all I focussed on each day; there was no looking to the future, reaching the next Friday's glass of wine, or booking the next holiday became all it was really about.

I speak to many people in the same position. Along the way, we lose sight of why we're doing what we're doing, why we're on that daily conveyor belt. And when that happens, it's very easy to become demotivated, unhappy, and not really sure why we're still doing it. Hence the "I'm not even sure I want to be a lawyer anymore" I hear from coaching clients so often.

Whatever your beliefs about life, we all need a purpose, a why. Even companies and businesses need a why to get up in the morning. What is your why?

What do you want life to look like in 3, 5, or 10 years' time? Thinking about your vision for your future can help. I encourage you to spend a little time thinking about it or writing about it if you like journaling. If you get stuck (as I did initially), I have recorded a great exercise I use in my workshops to get people thinking about their future. You can find the "ideal day" exercise on my website.

The "ideal day" exercise encourages you to think about how you'd like your day to look, although it is a normal working day. Importantly it focuses on how you are feeling on that ideal day. When something we want is attached to an emotion, i.e., we feel how it would feel to have that thing/to reach that goal, it's much more powerful than simply deciding we want something arbitrarily, maybe writing it down, but not really feeling anything about that goal. Like your targets maybe?

Whether you set targets for yourself or your employer sets them, how connected emotionally do you feel to those targets, and how enthusiastically do you feel about pursuing them? Attaching to the emotion means you are more likely to be motivated and enthusiastic. This is a useful tool, especially if you're feeling disillusioned at work or in your career. Focussing on why you're doing it can help you move through a difficult patch, and sometimes you can come to enjoy it again or get to a place you make decisions from if you decide to make a change.

For an example of this personal motivation versus set targets in practice, I'll share the story of a coaching client of mine. He was a six years qualified family lawyer, and in one session, we were working on his time recording.

He had got himself into the habit of under-recording, especially where he liked the client and was concerned about the rising costs of their matter. It was not a fixed fee issue; he simply put his concern for his client over his time recording. His firm was asking him to record more time. He was working longer hours into the evening and on weekends to make up the time, therefore losing time with his young family.

Simply telling him to record more time wasn't really working. Lawyers are clever people; if simply telling us what to do isn't working, something else is probably going on under the surface (probably not even consciously known about) stopping us. In his case, his compassion for his clients (which was really admirable) kept holding him back; he didn't want to be "that sort" of lawyer who only cared about the time or money and not about the client. Do you hear the story he was telling himself about the person he wanted to be, but how that was trapping him in longer working hours and getting constant requests from management to increase his chargeable time.

We explored "being a nice person" and how he's looking after his clients were having a detrimental impact on his family time and his enjoyment and enthusiasm for his work.

By finding his motivation for his work, to provide for his family, we reframed chargeable time into something that supported his loved ones (and was not solely for the benefit of his clients, who, let's face it, could choose any lawyer they want to and are unlikely to put him and his family before any of their own interests).

The moral of this story is to go to your motivation. What positive feeling are you working towards, and what is your why?

Use this to fuel attaining your targets rather than simply I must do this, or my boss, senior partner, or accountant will be on my back.

Think BIG

When working on your vision, don't limit yourself. Don't set parameters around what is "reasonable" or "likely." Dream BIG!

The ideal day exercise is excellent for this as it allows you to access the subconscious part of your brain, which allows you to dream rather than simply your logical, rational thinking part. This isn't about the "how"; leave that for later.

For now, I ask you to dream as big as your dare. This book contains lots of small steps you can take towards achieving that dream, but it's helpful for you to have an idea of what that looks like in the first place.

We all need a direction, or we are just on that conveyor belt. We need a focus point to be heading towards. One of my dear business buddies, Marianne Page, says in her book "Simple Logical Repeatable" that it's like getting into our car with no map, address or sat nav. Without a destination, we are just driving aimlessly around. This is great for a leisurely Sunday drive, but we can't live our lives and careers this way. A legal career has been pretty good at laying out that conveyor belt for us, but is it time to step off and see what we want? In the next Chapter we start looking at why it might be time to think a little differently.

Chapter 6.

Culture in Law

"Stress shouldn't be part and parcel
of the job.
No one should be leaving the
profession they trained for years to
join, because they can't reconcile
their career with their life."

– HANNAH BEKO

I s the old model of law broken?

Yes, I think it is, and perhaps it's time to take a good look at how we need to change. Here's a brief list of why I believe this is the case, and we'll look at some of these in more detail in this Chapter.

Our current system is hundreds of years old and really not fit for purpose. Many firms still work on the profits per equity partner (PEP) structure. This way of working requires lawyers below the equity level to work hard in exchange for the promise of equity partnership in the future – where the real money is made and where the power to make decisions and bring about change really sits in that firm.

The PEP system itself is flawed, in my opinion. As I've mentioned earlier in this book, although hotly contested by some, we lawyers are a service industry. Without providing a service to clients, there would be no law firm; there would be no profits. The PEP system thrives on charging clients as much as possible and paying the lawyers delivering that service as little as possible. This maximises revenue for the equity partners.

I've also heard it said that one of the reasons law firms are so profitable is that lawyers aren't paid overtime. Yet will very frequently (in fact, I'd hazard a guess 80-90% of the time) work more than their contracted hours.

One senior lawyer told me proudly how she'd negotiated to finish at 3 pm a few days a week to pick her children up from school and spend the afternoon with them. A year into that role, she told me she was logging on and working another 3 hours in the evening. But, she was only paid until 3 pm each day. I asked her to work out how many hours she was working pro-rata over the month and divide this by her annual salary; what hourly rate was she actually earning? Not a lawyer's salary, that's for certain!

Does working non-equity staff so hard result in the best service for clients or in the happiness and fulfilment of the lawyers servicing those clients? I don't think so.

Can this model continue for another 100 years? No, I don't believe it can or that it will. (This comment was written before the global pandemic!)

There are a number of lawyers out there who still aspire to the lofty heights of equity partnership, and they will no doubt continue the system for now in some firms.

But, those numbers are diminishing. The so-called "millennials" or "gen z" we're told don't want it (and I don't blame them), and many senior lawyers are taking the decision that equity partnership, or any partner title, involves too much of a sacrifice to their health, wellbeing and family time. Senior lawyers are leaving the profession at higher levels than ever, and this isn't only women. I am working with more and more male lawyers deciding the law isn't good for their health.

Adding to this Chapter post-pandemic, I believe the irreversible changes we've now seen. Early into the pandemic, I was interviewed by Matt Smeed, Business Psychologist, about the impact on the legal profession. Matt asked whether a lawyer's values had changed as a result of the pandemic. I don't believe values have been changed, but I believe they have been "realised." Many of us have been driven by values such as success, wealth, and achievement since our young school days. But from my conversations (including on my #FridayConversations, the law in lockdown, and beyond podcast), many lawyers and other professionals have realised that they value family, home, their health, etc. more than perhaps they had realised or given time and energy to in the past. I don't think this will change. Law firms will need to adapt to retain those lawyers (and attract new talent) with these "new" values.

The 6 Minute Unit

The 6-minute unit and charging by the hour is archaic and should be replaced. Interestingly I looked into how the 6-minute unit and the billable hour came about. I'd assumed this was by reference to some industrial revolution throwback equating legal professionals to machines required to produce a certain output during their working day. But, I discovered that the long-used and much-debated practice appears to have originated around 1914 in Boston, US. Reginald Heber Smith had attempted to run a large number of legal aid cases on a low budget and introduced the 6-minute unit and time recording to reduce costs and get through more cases.

"Actually, nothing could be simpler than a form on which you wrote the name of the client, the name of the case (because a client may have several cases in the office at the same time), and a brief description of the work you did, and the time you spent doing it."

"This simple plan had but one weakness: lawyers are individualists," Smith wrote. "They hate any system, and to keep a detailed record of time seemed to them about as bad as a slave system."

Isn't it interesting that so many years later, we are still using a system that was originally created by Smith for internal planning and budgeting and, even in its early years, was seen to have a negative impact on the lawyer's personal lives? Health and sanity!

When I tell law students or anyone outside law about the 6-minute unit, they think it's crazy!

Yes, I am biased. I haven't needed to time record for over ten years, saving myself over an hour a day just clicking that carpe diem timer on and off and allocating it to matters at the end of the day.

Increasingly clients don't care what our hourly rates are or how many units we've recorded. They want their job done as quickly and effectively as possible and to know (as far as reasonably possible).

I've heard of a one-time recording system that sits at the top of the screen, permanently counting down the required six chargeable hours. It stays on red until the lawyer reaches the required 6 hours and then turns green. It's no wonder lawyers' stress levels are so high when they are constantly monitoring their time and justifying themselves and the burden of always being accurate and efficient.

I can only imagine the psychological impact this little red timer has on those lawyers, and I would even go so far as to predict that if you measured the cortisol levels (stress hormone) of those lawyers, I would expect they might be higher in that firm than in others! (Does it help with productivity? I'd love access to the figures; I suspect it's exactly the opposite of what they are trying to achieve).

The competing requirements for lawyers simply aren't compatible. The 6-minute unit and time recording generally, combined with daily, monthly, and annual targets for hours, billing, write-off, and utilisation, simply isn't in the client's best interests or that of the lawyer. They probably only serve the law firm, and then only to a point.

Whilst the law firm wants the lawyer to record as many hours as they can per day, have their utilisation as high as possible, and their write off as low as possible, this leads to unhelpful behaviours such as time dumping on files or under-recording because you know you're already over your estimate given to the client. Suppose the time is not recoverable by not recording it. In that case, the lawyer doesn't need to have that uncomfortable conversation with their boss about a write-off, or is it a training or experience gap, or simply something they have not come across before, or an argumentative opponent, or a demanding client?

There are 101 reasons more time is recorded on a matter than is recoverable. When individuals have issues with perfectionism and/or imposter syndrome, they are also under time recording, believing that they are not as good or as fast as their peers. But, whilst the lawyer has this "fear" in the back of their mind, they are left working extra hours each week to make up for the time they have decided not to record and using their valuable energy to make these sorts of value judgements decisions all day long.

This is why I say it only benefits the law firm to a point. They do not have their lawyers working at their optimum efficiency. They are not getting through as much work, and perhaps even not as accurately, whilst they have all of these other concerns running around in their head.

And what of the client whose business we exist to serve? They want their job done as quickly and efficiently as possible and at the lowest possible cost. Time recording and the 6-minute unit certainly don't benefit them.

We have seen a hybrid system for some years now where clients are given a fixed fee for many non-litigious matters, but time is still recorded. This effectively is then used as a measure (or a stick) against the lawyer. If the client's fee is fixed (bar anything untoward or additional unforeseen circumstances appearing), why record time at all? Just use the time it takes to put the timers on and off and record it to the matter etc. (it all adds up to quite a lot of time in a day) to progress the client matter and get it finished as swiftly as possible.

Many forward-thinking firms, not only the fee share/self-employment models, are working on reducing or abolishing time recording. If you're in a position now or in the future to consider this, I recommend you take the plunge and try. Don't forget to measure the client satisfaction, employee engagement and wellbeing levels, productivity, and overall profitability before and afterward!

The Coat on the Chair

Presenteeism has to change. Lawyers are highly trained professionals. The idea that they can't be trusted to do their work when someone can't see them makes me angry. I'm encouraged to see some firms making big changes in this area. One Manchester firm's new offices (pre-pandemic) has desks for half of their staff, making working from home compulsory for about half of the week. Of course, in editing this chapter post-2020/2021, there are likely to be a great many more firms reducing their office space. But of course, that's not to say we don't see presenteeism even when people are working at home. Have you come across the article about lasers being used to monitor when people are away from their desks?!

Jessica Swannell, practice manager and costs lawyer at A&M Bacon in Peterborough, shared with me in 2019 how she had implemented flexible working and increased billable hours from 3-5 per day to 6-7 per day. Multiply that by the number of lawyers and the number of days in a month, and you get a lot of extra billable hours.

If you were running a business (maybe you are), wouldn't you like to increase output that much at no extra cost to you (and perhaps even see a cost reduction?) You could save money on the smaller office space and fewer facilities and save the environment by having fewer cars on the road. (You can tell this was pre-pandemic, but at a time where we are seeing firms find their feet with more flexible working, we still need to be mindful of looking for the right balance.

I know I can be a complete bore when it comes to extolling the virtues of flexible working. Besides it saving the firm money and improving the environment, it's shown in study after study to increase employees' enjoyment and sense of fulfilment in their work.

People have a better sense of "balance" simply from walking their kids to school once or twice a week or being at home when their teenagers get back from college.

The pandemic has, in some ways, caused some damage to my argument about the benefits of flexibility and more working from home due to its impact on mental health than to the extent that we can blame only working from home and not the plethora of other concerns around at that time. In a forced situation, many have found working from home 100% of the time to be detrimental to their health.

Of course, doing anything 100% of the time is not good for us. There needs to be moderation, like with many other things. For the first three years of my own legal business, I worked from home almost all of the time, and it certainly played a part in my increasing stress levels. Not taking a break, getting any exercise or fresh air, and not being around other people, weren't good for me. Once I realised it had a negative impact, I started varying the routine so that I'd work at least one day a week in one of the offices and one in a coffee shop. This is still my favourite way to work.

Post pandemic, we are seeing something similar playing out. There will be those who want to be in the office every day and those who, over time, find a balance of both office and home, which works for them. We may start to see changes in the work-life balance and stress culture if this shift is here to stay. I hope firms will support more choices for employees in the coming years.

Why should a business care about the sense of balance their employees feel, apart from it being a good thing to care about the welfare of staff? Happy staff are more productive and take fewer sick days. They are less likely to suffer from stress or depression, resulting in long work absences. The business could become the firm of choice which means they get the pick of the good candidates. It's a win-win as far as I'm concerned.

Surveys show that the ability to work flexibly impacts happiness more than a pay rise! I must caveat that by flexible working, I don't mean working from home because you're having a washing machine delivered. I mean genuine flexible working that is promoted, encouraged, and supported by good remote IT that actually works. All of this is far more achievable now.

There is a final point I'd like to raise about flexibility and working from home post-pandemic. Some firms and organisations may never accept a flexible approach and may still prefer to see their lawyers in the office. I encourage you as an individual to consider what really works best for you and perhaps for your family. Don't forget what a family needs changes over time as well. There is no "one and done" here.

Very often, we lawyers become institutionalised. We can become so used to doing things a certain way that it seems wrong or scary to do it differently. The way we have always done things has led to the profession ranking at the top of the list of stressful professions, higher than average rates of anxiety, depression, and reliance on alcohol, and a large attrition rate.

The way we have been doing it isn't working.
What would work best for you?

Millennials or Gen Z Difference

There is a lot of talk about the impact of new entrants into the law. Generally considered to be those born between the early 1980s to the mid-1990s, which only just excludes me!

The general rhetoric is that millennials don't want to work the same gruelling hours and sacrifice so much of their free time, health, and wellbeing as those more senior might have done. I don't have statistics on this phenomenon, and I raise it more as a point of discussion than a definitive truth. In fact, over the past couple of years, I've come to see that the real changes might be seen first through Gen Z, who were born from the 2000s onwards and are now our law students and training lawyers.

My generation still tends to be fairly unwilling to challenge the system of long hours and lack of autonomy, but from what I see of the Gen Z lawyers, I think firms will need to change their thinking.

If the stories are to be believed, the old systems won't work for those who are more conscious of their own wellbeing and happiness, and that may be no bad thing.

I speak to 5-10 year PQE lawyers who tell me they see the hours their senior partners put in and their sacrifices, and they don't want to do it. It will be interesting to see how this develops and impacts the profession – although it may be some years yet before we see significant change.

Many of our current more senior lawyers came through the ranks expecting eventually to make it to the higher levels, either for the salary, the managerial responsibility, or the career satisfaction. But the job takes its toll, and not everyone will get there. Or they decide on the way that it's not worth it.

This is a shame as these individuals might make great managers or partners. Do we really want only those who don't priories work-life balance in the top positions? (See Chapter 9 on Leaders in Law).

"I don't want to be management, to be a partner," I hear some say. And for some, that might be true. For others, once we delve a little deeper into their reasoning, it's because of the perceived sacrifices they believe it will take. They see those who have gone before them, and that puts them off. If there were more "role models" doing it in a different way, would more want to go for these opportunities, I wonder?

I have to ask, how many lawyers don't want a leadership role? Or is the truth that they don't want a leadership role the way they've seen it done until now?

A lawyer's beliefs

A trainee solicitor coaching client shared a number of beliefs in our first session together.

These beliefs were:

- working in the law demands that you work long hours;
- you always need to be busy; and
- there is no room for weakness (and weakness relates here to not being able to "do it all."

She was less than a year into her journey within the law, and to hear her make these comments as though they were statements of fact made me very glad she was working with me!

When you read these statements, do you agree that we must accept these facts?   Or that whilst this might be what we've experienced in the past, they don't have to be or to remain true?

I've included an exercise in the resources section of the website to help you to take a closer look at some of your lawyer/legal career-related beliefs if they are not the most useful or empowering (or just downright stress-inducing).

A few final thoughts on changing the culture

From this chapter, you'll have seen that I'm an advocate for leaving behind the chargeable hours model. It doesn't adequately reward lawyers for the extras they bring to the table. The "soft skills" that are so necessary and not just a nice to have. Training both technical and vital behavioural skills, together with supervision and pastoral care of team members, are all vital and not properly recognised and supported in the chargeable hours/utilisation model.

Law firms are profitable because of all of the overtime the lawyers work for free. Whilst I'm well aware that we need to provide an excellent service to our clients and can't leave them mid completion etc., we all can be guilty of working on into the evenings, at the weekends and when we are on holiday. We do this, in my opinion, out of fear of the consequences if we don't. We won't be seen as favourably as Joe Bloggs at our next review; our commitment to our firm or our work might be questioned, and our bonus might be affected. If it's our own business (as I know all too well), we worry about losing clients and the impact that might have on our income and ability to pay the mortgage. I'd like us to recognise that this overwork comes from a place of fear and enquire into just how true those fears are. We all need to be braver and say when enough is enough, a journey I'm still very much on myself.

Start to look for this fear-based reaction in yourself. Ask yourself:

a) what's the worst that could happen? (lose client, lose job, lose house, etc.)

b) what's the best that could happen? (I could get promoted due to the outstanding work-life balance role modelling I am demonstrating)

c) what's most likely to happen? (probably absolutely nothing at all, except you make it home to share dinner with your friends/family, feel more satisfied in your work, perhaps even perform a little better as a result, and don't quit?!)

Lawyers tend to look for the downsides to see the worst-case scenario without over generalizing. We're paid to do this for our clients. But, it's not helpful when assessing our career and life choices. I urge you to look for what's most likely to happen rather than what's the worst that could happen, and make your decisions from this place.

Yes, a male/female distinction comes in here as well. Generally speaking, although not exclusively, women take on more of the pastoral roles resulting in lower recorded time at pay/bonus review time which enhances the gender pay gap. This sort of activity need not be reserved just for women, and those men who've read my Authenticity Chapter will be well placed to take on some of these roles.

I know some great male lawyers who already are. Neither men nor women should be penalised in their pay/bonus or promotion prospects for taking on these important duties. It's time we valued the whole lawyer and not only the part which is billing the client.

Again the pandemic has accelerated thinking in this area as pastoral care (never something on the agenda) is now a key feature in leadership and management training.

In the next chapter, we will look at one of the fundamental reasons why changing the culture in law is so vital.

Chapter 7.

Mental Health in Law

"95% of lawyers surveyed reported suffering from moderate to severe work-related stress in a study of over 8,000 conducted by The Law Society in 2015."

THE AUTHENTIC LAWYER 2022

- **A 1990 Johns Hopkins University study of over 100 professions found lawyers to be at the top of the charts for depression**

- **58% of junior lawyers had considered taking time off work for mental health reasons but did not do so, and 14% of junior lawyers had suicidal thoughts, according to research in 2019 by the Junior Lawyers Division.**

I couldn't write this book (authentically) without including this Chapter, given the quite horrifying statistics relating to lawyers' mental health. I've touched on mental health several times throughout earlier Chapters. For example, when inadequate support and supervision are available and where character armour and masks are worn to protect us from judgment and rejection.

One of the main reasons behind the mental health statistics is often cited as the pressure of work. For me, this brings in several elements we have been discussing in this book. Confidence gaps, fears of judgment or failure, lack of effective delegation, people-pleasing, and inability to say no contribute to poor mental health.

Let me clarify what I mean by mental health. Included (but not limited to) diagnosed conditions such as anxiety, burnout, depression, and fatigue. But also chronic stress, which many lawyers do not even realise they are going through. It often goes unrealised that symptoms such as headaches, back and neck aches, and stomach upsets are caused by stress.

Common symptoms of stress include:

- Having trouble getting to sleep at night; shoulder, neck, or back pain or stomach ache/sickness.
- Often waking in the night around 2-3 am preoccupied with what you've forgotten to do or may have done wrong.
- Struggling with focus and concentration.
- Memory is not as good as eating too much or too little.
- drinking too much; or
- "Silly" things keep happening, like getting a speeding ticket or minor bumps in the car, something that might be out of character for you normally.

Once I'd reversed my car into stationary objects three times in less than a year, I realised I was clearly not giving the road its attention. Should I even be driving my children around?   But the lesson I needed to learn from this experience was that I was rushing about, trying to do everything myself, and had a mind that was too full of work to concentrate on what was right in front of me.

Do you ever notice yourself feeling cynical, demotivated, exhausted from work demands, and sleepless at night? That's the definition of burnout.

Interestingly the origins of the term burnout in 1974 came from psychologist Herbert Freudenberger who worked as a volunteer at a drug treatment clinic. He noticed these burnout symptoms in his team of rehabilitation centre volunteers. I find it fascinating that a syndrome originally found in caregivers is so prevalent in the legal profession (and increasing) that I suspect this would surprise many people outside of the law.

But, the profession has many qualities which make us uniquely placed to suffer from burnout. We are a service industry (I know some people disagree), but we sometimes serve very demanding clients.

And we do this in an environment of pressure, the chargeable hour, utilisation, write-off, and billing targets, to mention only a few. Many lawyers also have traits that make burnout more likely, being people-pleasers, struggling with the word no, and not being great at putting our own needs before those of others – be it our clients, our team, our boss, or our families.

For my part, the edges of burnout looked like this:

- Chronic stress affects my decision-making, making it almost impossible to think rationally.
- A total inability to switch off from work and my business;
- Frequently waking at 2-3 am running over what I needed to do and trying to remember what I'd forgotten; and
- catastrophising over very little thing that could be perceived as "wrong."

I remember a lawyer friend sharing with me that when she was finally signed off with depression, she was awake every night mentally auditing her files to find that one thing she'd done wrong. This is exactly how I felt in the midst of my chronic stress and being on the edge of burnout.

Sometimes burnout can be seen only by looking backward. It often hits us after we have achieved the thing.

Do you ever find yourself struggling until you go away on holiday and then find you're poorly? The adrenalin carries us through until we take our foot off the pedal. Burnout sneaks up in a similar way.

Reaching partnership was a trigger for my husband. He says, looking backward, reaching what at the time he considered to be the pinnacle of his career, his long-term ambition, was the start of his burnout. Now he sees that after the excitement and pride of that achievement, he started to feel demotivated and lost interest in his work.

For me, the final straw was suffering from panic attacks when my then two-year-old slept upstairs, and I had a business to run. I knew I had to do something to be the Mum I wanted to be so that I didn't lose everything I'd worked so hard for.

I needed to change, and I needed to change completely and for the long term, not just for a few months and not by tinkering around the edges. I still look back and say that as hard as this period of my life was, it was the best thing that could have happened to me.

In 2015 there was a new case of depression or anxiety diagnosed every 2 minutes. This sounds bad enough, but there are many more unreported and even unrealised cases out there, especially in law. Whether it's burnout or depression, many lawyers are on the scale, have been, or will be if they carry on the way they are. Many of my coaching clients might be aware that they are on the scale of depression but don't want to have anything such as anxiety or depression showing on their medical notes for fear that it might impact their career.

I'm not medically trained and can't profess to be able to diagnose depression or anxiety, but I've learned to look for the tell-tale signs and train team leaders and managers to do the same.

I use a profiling tool with my coaching clients, and common results seen by those approaching the borderline of depression are a distinct lack of self-esteem, little or no time dedicated to taking care of themselves, experiencing life as grey or monotone, feeling joy infrequently, often feeling laden with rules and discipline (us lawyers really?!)

Sadly, these traits not only indicate deep unhappiness and lack of self-esteem, but they frequently mean a lack of creativity. Creativity and problem solving can be so useful in our profession.

The big issues I see currently in our profession regarding mental health are:

1. It's almost a badge of honour to be so busy that you can only just cope. Working long hours to the point of exhaustion has always been seen as an achievement, something to be proud of.

2. Have you ever had one of those conversations over who stayed up the latest on a completion, how many hours you've worked that week, or what your utilisation is? The truth is that firms have perpetuated competitiveness in the past. Groups of similarly qualified fee earners were regularly pitted against each other in terms of their hours and billing targets.

3. Character armour prevents us from being who we really are. Being someone else, acting a part, is tiring, but we get so good at it that we're doing it 24/7 until we forget who WE really are beyond the title we have at work.

4. Over the past few years, there has been a noticeable increase in the conversations around mental health; we have mental health first aiders and charters. The

huge stigma around being able to cope with stress; hence it being under-reported for fear that it will end your career. To admit that we're struggling is perceived as being weak. To an extent, the stigma is reducing, but we do need to see effective strategies put in place for managing and reducing stress and safeguarding the well-being and not just more of an openness to admit when we're struggling.

5. Some evidence that it does end careers. I hasten to add that I believe this is self-inflicted. By this, I mean that the lawyer involved decides to opt-out as they feel unable to continue or to return after a break. Suppose we accept (as I think we should) that something approaching 100% of lawyers will struggle with chronic stress, anxiety, depression and/or burnout at some point in their career. In that case, we can change the conversation from whether or not we are suffering and instead make it about how we can change things for everyone.

6. Common traits in lawyers that (again, only my opinion) predispose us to be more likely to suffer from mental health-related issues such as perfectionism, people-pleasing, and imposter syndrome, all of which we delved into in the Character Traits Chapter.

7. A tendency towards a fixed rather than a growth mindset. With a fixed mindset, we tend to believe that this is the way things are; we can't change. On the other hand, a growth mindset looks for ways to grow and improve. Carol Dweck (who you will find on YouTube) talks about the difference between these mindsets. Although I see green shoots in the profession where we are talking more and more about mental health and wellbeing, I fear we are creating a new culture where it's okay to say we are struggling and to opt-out, not necessarily to seize the chance to positively address it.

It's just my opinion that:

a) most lawyers will go through some form of mental health issue in their career, if not all of them; and

b) seeking help, whether that might be medical or alternative, does not make a person weak. In fact, it makes them brave, and they will come out of the process a stronger person.

I'd really like us to see any exploration of our mental health and wellbeing as a valuable and worthwhile exercise. When someone says they are going to complete a physical challenge, train for a marathon or a 10k, complete a triathlon, we wish them well, we sponsor them. How could we start approaching mental fitness in the same way?

Knowing how to manage your mental health these days is a key skill and whether we develop it because we are on the floor and have no choice or because we decide to develop these skills before that happens, it's my mission to encourage lawyers and firms to drop the stigma and see this work as positive and necessary.

Some parting thoughts on mental health:
- Stress does not have to be part and parcel of the job;
- Antidepressants are sometimes needed, but not always. There are some excellent alternatives to the medical route (although if you feel you may need medical help, please do visit your GP). Meditation, for example, has been shown in some studies to be as effective as antidepressants, and it certainly was my saviour in 2015 and again in the pandemic;
- Don't ever feel alone or suffer in silence; although it's extremely sad that the profession suffers so badly with stress and mental health, it means there is always someone who understands exactly how you feel and can listen with a supporting ear. I highly recommend LawCare, the mental health charity for

the legal profession, and also becoming part of any peer support groups you can; and

- Men and women in our profession can experience chronic stress and other mental health issues. In many ways, it's the great equaliser. We will go on to look at this further in the next Chapter.

Useful resources

- I share a simple and easy to use meditation with you in the free downloads section of my website. Other simple techniques to help relieve stress include, getting some exercise and fresh air, breathing deeply, setting aside a little time just for you even if it's half an hour at the weekend to spend some time alone reading, writing, listening to music, or taking a walk.

-

- And finally – no one needs to feel alone. We can break the stigma by talking honestly and openly about mental health in law. Find a community or network that you trust. You're welcome to join my Facebook community for members of the legal profession, you'll find a link in the resources section of my website.

Chapter 8

Men and Women in Law

> **"**
>
> "I always wondered, "why somebody doesn't do something about that?" until I realised I was that somebody. "
>
> ---
>
> – LILY TOMLIN

Not long ago, we celebrated 100 years of women being able to practise law. In contrast, men have been practising since an estimated 1190, that's over 830 years!

Before we dive into the men and women in law discussion, I want to make clear that whilst I am a woman in the law, my husband is also a lawyer, and I have three boys. This book is (I hope) to be read by men and women, and in my coaching and training consultancy, I also work with both. We, women, need our male allies, and we actually have far more challenges in common than we might have originally realised.

According to the Law Society, women have been entering the profession in larger numbers than men for quite some time.

There are numbers of new entries to the roll, but numbers of women in practice start to decrease around 8-10 years qualified, most likely, due to the family career juggle, although not always exclusively. Over the last couple of years, I have seen an increasing number of men and women leaving the profession due to the toll taken on their mental health and well-being. Although it might have appeared more socially acceptable for women to choose to leave the profession (to opt-out) than for men, I have an increasing number of male coaching clients who are wondering if they will stay in law much longer.

I expect this change to increase in the coming years, partly due to the pandemic's toll on people and the realisation of what's important to them. If their firm (or they may decide the law as a whole) can't accommodate their re-assessed life values, leaving might seem like the only option.

As a side note, I am not a fan of everyone leaving the profession as a first option. I believe very often, with a look at what isn't working for that person and exploring all of the many and varied options out there now, there can be an enjoyable and satisfying career in law for many. I would encourage anyone feeling like this to potentially reach out to a coach or a really good recruiter to explore their options before making a big decision.

However, the startling fact remains that whilst larger numbers of women than men are entering the profession, only around 15% of equity partnerships are held by women. What's going wrong? Firstly women don't feel encouraged or inspired to follow the path to partnership or equity if they don't see someone "like them" holding those positions.

If their role model for equity partnership is a woman who perhaps doesn't have a family, had a stay-at-home husband, or a full-time nanny, then other women coming after her who have perhaps made different lifestyle choices don't always feel that they can follow in her footsteps.

Many women (and some men) tell me they don't want to be a partner. When we dig into that decision, it is usually not that they don't want to be involved in the business or in the managing of clients or staff. Still, they don't want to make the perceived sacrifices to their life, family, health, or sanity that they believe partnership demands. I worry about how many excellent managers and business leaders we might be losing out on.

Whilst I have included a Chapter on Leaders in Law in this book, I delve further into coaching tips and skills for leaders inside Effective Practice Group Leadership published by Globe Law and Business, and you can find a link to this text on the website.

Unconscious bias

In 2018 the Law Society led by Christina Blacklaws carried out a series of round table discussions under the Women in Leadership in Law project. Following an earlier survey into the main barriers resulting in so few women holding leadership positions, over 225 roundtable discussions were held.

The greatest factor found to be impacting the progression of women in law was unconscious bias. I confess a term that I'd never really heard widely used before the roundtable discussions, or I confess really understood. We are all affected by unconscious bias, whether we are a 50-year-old male lawyer interviewing a prospective junior associate or a 25-year-old female lawyer applying for a job. We all have our perceived ideas about women, our roles, capabilities, and limitations.

There is, of course, scientific and biological evidence that women are different from men; you just have to look at our bodies and our brain! Physically, mentally and hormonally, we are different. So what?

For us, all in the profession to carry on acting as if everyone is the same has got women 15% of the way towards equality, with around 50% leaving the profession after eight years of practice.

To acknowledge men and women are different is not to say that they don't each bring something to the party in terms of being an effective lawyer, supervisor, or equity partner.

Our own internal unconscious bias will be slow to change like many things in law (likened to turning an oil tanker), but it doesn't mean we shouldn't make a start. We can do that in part by acknowledging this unconscious bias exists and without blaming anyone or any sections of the profession.

As a white, middle-aged lawyer, my husband certainly feels the finger is being pointed directly at him if such topics are raised, and that can't be helpful for us to bring about change. Can we all be on the lookout for such bias (in ourselves and inside our teams and organisations), be brave enough to look out for it, and also challenge our own thinking when it comes up. There should be no immediate assumptions made about what women (or indeed anyone, whether parents or not) might want out of their careers. Every person is different and what they want from their career is different at different times in their lives.

Masculine & Feminine

I use these terms rather than men and women for a specific reason. Generally speaking, women tend to display more of the traits that might be called feminine, and men tend to display more of the characteristics we might consider masculine. Men do not only show masculine characteristics and women-only feminine ones; each of us is made up of a mix of the two.

However, as we will discuss here, I believe it is useful and, in fact, necessary for a great lawyer to utilise both masculine and feminine behaviours in their careers and lives.

The law has, of course, been traditionally masculine. I would go so far as to say very masculine compared to other professions. Masculine traits tend to focus on competition, ambition, drive, tunnel vision, individualism, and the power of one. It is no surprise if men have been in the profession for 820 years longer than women and have had over 700 years to create its structure, systems, and ways of working before women (dressed and acting as men) came along.

Feminine traits tend to centre around collaboration, community, empathy, and the power of the group. The more masculine characteristics have been prevalent throughout the legal profession's history and are still dominant in many firms to a fairly large extent.

The historic rhetoric has been that feminine traits are weaker in some way. They are not so useful or even detrimental to a legal career. When I started out as a trainee, I noticed that the female partners were more like men than the men! I'm sure that it was no accident we had entered a male-dominated profession, and we felt the need to prove that we could do it just as well as the men. In the past, I suspect these women were probably right, and they wouldn't have received promotions if those in charge of the decision-making didn't see something of themselves in those they were promoting. (one of the classic traits of unconscious bias is only hiring or promoting people who are like you).

Times are changing, and you now see many women in the law happily displaying more of themselves (the central theme of this book, of course) in their everyday work and being promoted on that basis.

There is still a way to go, including those men in our profession who also feel that they don't fit into the stereotypical view of a male lawyer and who have the empathy, compassion, and self-awareness we so badly need in leadership roles.

The really interesting point here is not about increasing the number of women leaders and encouraging more to embrace feminine characteristics rather than being one of the men. The really interesting point for me is how men can and, in my view, should embrace more of their feminine characteristics. It's inauthentic to force a large amount of masculinity to be "one of the lads" if that's not someone's true nature. I feel this idea of masculine and feminine really impacts mental health, well-being, happiness, and what is expected of them.

Many of the male lawyers I've coached have struggled with this stereotypical lawyer image. They don't feel they fit easily into the world of constant competition, always being the best or the loudest. Male lawyers without a very strong masculine character (which is probably quite a large number) also feel sometimes that they are in the wrong career and can't truly be themselves.

How can we embrace more of the traditionally feminine characteristics as a good, useful, and maybe even vital part of our legal careers? Empathy, understanding, and a willingness to really listen, for example, are key skills for management training, client and staff retention, and employee satisfaction. I'd like to see more emphasis at the management level on these important characteristics. This would benefit the mental health of the person doing the management and provide stronger leadership in the teams they are responsible for.

A lovely heart centred and soul-driven lawyer shared with me about her training in the corporate department with a boss who was very difficult to work for. This boss's high levels of masculinity made it an unbearable place to work, and staff turnover was extremely high. The environment was so toxic that this lawyer needed to take time away from work due to the pressure and demands. I'm pleased to say that this didn't put the lawyer off a corporate career, and she's now working in a fantastic position and acts as a role model for those suffering in a toxic work environment.

Looking at this compassionately, I feel that this boss struggled with her own situation as a woman in a man's world. But those insecurities and pressures shouldn't be inflicted on her team, effectively making them ill.

If there were a little less toxic environment and a little more authenticity, things might be very different.
I would like to mention another aspect of female leadership as it is still present in some firms. Occasionally there is an attitude that "I had it hard, so you should too."

The chronic stress in the legal profession has a notable effect on fertility, very sadly. In the past, women promoted to partnership may not have had families, either as a conscious decision that they wanted to advance their career first, or perhaps not from choice. If they had a family, they might have had to sacrifice spending time with them. Many aspiring and current female partners do not want that particular lifestyle. They are ambitious and want partnership but not at the expense of their family or future family.

The tide is changing, even more so since the pandemic, but I fear in some places, it is "pushing the buttons" for want of a better phrase, of more senior partners who perhaps find that hard to reconcile with their own lives and past decisions.

Maybe they didn't sacrifice family life but instead sacrificed who they really were/their true nature to reach their career goal.

As we've seen with unconscious bias, we unintentionally or perhaps intentionally hire and promote people who are like us. More traditional firms appointing partners would be looking for female partners who displayed very similar traits to their existing male partnership.

I coached a wonderful lawyer in her late 40s who was very experienced, had excellent relationships with her clients and had a successful practice. But she felt lost and didn't know who she was. She'd spent her entire career fitting in and being what and who she believed others expected. You might wonder why this matters if she is doing well, but our titles and income aren't the only measures of how well we are doing in life. This lawyer is so much more than her career alone, like all of us. Her health, personal life, and happiness were all being held back as she worked so hard to carry on the pretence about who she was.

I talk more about the impact of being authentic in Chapter 2, but here I want to leave you with this thought - if you find yourself working in a toxic environment that doesn't support your dreams and goals, it may be time to look elsewhere - if you aren't able to influence change within your firm.

If you're in a position of leadership, ask yourself:
a) Are you supportive of colleagues around you even if they are not the "same" as you?
b) Even if you found it hard to rise through the ranks, do you look to make it easier for those coming behind you?
c) Do you role model those traits which are natural to you rather than traits that you see in everyone else?

I would like to reiterate that it's not only women who feel the need to emulate traits previously demonstrated by those ahead of them. Many male lawyers bend themselves and their personalities to fit in. This is likely to negatively affect their mental health, well-being, achievements, and overall satisfaction and tends to be one of the biggest issues I see in my male lawyer clients.

When researching for my piece on Practice Group Leaders, I spoke with a senior male partner who had previously managed over 150 lawyers. He described his role as being that of a shield, effectively "protecting" his team from the pressures of the firm. I could hear the toll this had taken on his mental health and well-being. No doubt, he was a great manager and a loss to the profession.

You can imagine my response when only the next week, a junior lawyer starting out on his management journey mentioned he felt as though he was a "shield" to his trainee and paralegal!

The Confidence Gap

In relation to female lawyers, it is often mentioned that they don't tend to have as much confidence as their male counterparts. This is frequently cited as the reason more women don't put themselves forward for promotion, and hence why we have such a gap at the top.

You may have heard the suggestion that men will go for a promotion when they believe they fulfill 60% of the criteria, but women will only go for a promotion when they fit 90% or even 100% of the criteria. Anecdotally I suspect this is quite true for female lawyers, certainly from the women I've coached and spoken to my recruiter friends about. On the criteria they would make excellent leadership material but they don't see it. A nice big mix of impostor syndrome, perfectionist, and that little bit of fear about what sort of person they would become or need to become in order to take on that role.

Somaya Ouazzani of Mimosa Fleur shared with me her frustration at seeing wonderful female candidates perfect for a role, but sometimes it's just a leap too far for them.

"Sabotaging mindsets are a very real thing amonst lawyers. It is these mindsets that have kept the lawyers I work with in a state of homeostatis. They know better but keep choosing to stay stuck.

As lawyers they are great at building their clients' cases, but they're also very good at building their own elaborate and convincing case against going for what they want and deserve, shrouding these cases around "logic" and "reason".

They shouldn't rock the boat to ask for that payrise. They don't want to upset the apple cart by asking for that promotion. They don't want to become unpopular amoungst management for raising issues around pressure, hours, culture.

Don't be afriad to claim what you deserve! Get out of an unhappy work life. Don't let it become stagnant. Don't let it get toxic. Go get what's yours."

Many female and male lawyers say they don't want a partnership role, although many others may see their potential. Of course, ultimately, it's a decision for that individual, but for my part, I'd like to see them spend a little time evaluating their reasoning behind not wanting a position that they may be excellently suited for. If it's out of fear that they have to change who they are and become someone they don't want to be, I'd say we need them all the more in those leadership roles, but exactly as they are and not changed into someone else.

The law needs more compassionate, team-driven, and empathetic leaders. We need to encourage and support the great lawyers who have those talents to step into that leadership role. I hope this book goes some way towards doing just that.

This book isn't about necessarily about equality – but here is a section just for the men!

Over the last few years, I've become more involved in the debate around female equality in law, ironically after I'd become a partner and actually wasn't impacted (or so I thought) by any gender imbalance between men and women in the law.

But in my life and home over the years, I've come to notice that imbalance, especially as my career grew.

My husband is also a commercial property lawyer (you can imagine our conversations over dinner!). We'd unwittingly fallen into that gender-stereotypical pattern of the women being the main carer, the fallback, the emergency cover when a child was ill.

I was 200 miles from home on a three-day conference on one such occasion. My phone was switched off, and my answerphone message said I was away. At around 6 pm, I picked up three messages from the school saying my son was poorly and needed to be collected. Of course, they eventually called my husband, but Mum is the first port of call, and it left me wondering if I needed to keep checking my phone all day even though I had recorded a message to say I was unavailable. I wonder if our male counterparts have to do the same?

The interesting part is the effect that this has had on my husband. My husband and I have had to confront this inequality for our family, our relationship, and my sanity. Now things have changed, and we work as a team.

He's now a 50:50 shareholder in the school drop-offs, and pickups, covering the sick days, making the pack lunches, and joining the school days out. I see the huge impact this has had on his sense of well-being and life satisfaction.

For many years he did what he thought a male lawyer should do. The long hours in the office, taking a second seat in family life. He says managing our 8-year-olds football team is one of the best things he's ever done! Being more authentic to himself and living more of the life he wants to live is an ongoing journey, but it's so good to see.

It's also, I think, the key to equality for women - when men share the responsibilities and are equally responsible for covering chickenpox and early morning drop-offs - the closer and closer we will come to true equality.

Chapter 9

Leaders in Law

> **"**
>
> "It continues to surprise me how many leaders attempt to be one way at work, while their "true" personality emerges outside of work... And it surprises me when these same leaders seem shocked or confused when their employees don't trust them, don't like them, and can't really wait to work elsewhere."

— KEVIN KRUSE

I
n this Chapter, I am not only talking about leaders in the traditional sense – those who might be the boss, head of a department, or the team leader. We are all leaders, whether it's the school PTA, the scouts, our secretary, paralegal, or trainee. As parents or godparents, we are role models to others. It's leadership in the wider sense that I'm talking about here. Wherever you are in your career, right at the beginning, or leading a team of 50, this is equally relevant.

The quote at the start of this Chapter is from NY Times bestselling author and serial entrepreneur Kevin Kruse and demonstrates beautifully how important authenticity is in our careers, even more so if we want to progress.

Traits of Authentic Leaders

- High levels of self-awareness and emotional intelligence. Not being afraid of emotions. We cover emotions in greater detail in the Authenticity Chapter.

- Being mission-driven, understanding that it's not only about you as an individual. When you're a leader (in whatever capacity), it is not only about your own income, position, money, ego, etc. It is about the collective, whether that's your organisation, your team, or your family unit. It's about putting the goals of the collective at the centre.

- Leading with the heart, not being afraid of emotions. We've probably all had bosses, who are almost robotic, and were difficult to talk to, difficult to approach and get to know. These are the sorts of leaders people don't like, don't trust, and don't really want to work with — we don't want to be that sort of leader!

In our post-pandemic world, we're going to need really great leaders. The above skills are going to become vitally important. Becoming more inclusive is going to be an important consideration for both managers and organisations themselves. As mentioned in Chapter 2, self-awareness is one of the key outstanding traits for effective leaders. Former US Law Firm HR manager (now executive coach for professionals) Laura Simpson says of the link between self-awareness and inclusivity: *Put simply, coaching drastically raises self-awareness. How can we see others and recognise their valuable contributions if we can't truly see ourselves?*

Very much along these lines, it's my belief that the inclusivity conversation requires bravery. Not being afraid of emotions, being able to talk to team members about how they're feeling, are struggling with the changes, and what the future holds? We need those who can learn not to fear vulnerability and genuine open connection.

What I find personally, having been on this journey for a few years. Is that the more open and vulnerable you can be with people (in the right situations using your common sense)? This creates a better and stronger connection, whether it's with your clients, your peers at work, or new contacts in a networking sense.

This vulnerability and connection piece allows you to stand out compared to others. This is why I refer to Authenticity as a Lawyer's Superpower!

Many lawyers will be too afraid to show any signs of emotion, vulnerability, or compassion to open up and be who they truly are with other people. Those who do will stand out from everyone else, whether it's in a leadership role, as part of a team, or whether it's in a business development/networking sense.

If being more courageous and vulnerable appeals to you, the very best place to start is with Brené Brown's work. Her TedTalk on Vulnerability is only 20 minutes long and has been viewed over 15 million times. It's a great place to start thinking about the fear and power of vulnerability, the courage to be imperfect, willing to let go of who we think we thought should be and who we are.

"Leadership is not about titles or the corner office. It's about the willingness to step up, put yourself out there, and lean into courage. The world is desperate for braver leaders. It's time for all of us to step up."
Brene Brown (Dare to Lead)

Brené Brown, in her book "Dare to Lead," believes leadership takes uncertainty, risk and a willingness to accept emotional exposure. Really great leaders are not afraid of showing their team when they are vulnerable. This is not about dumping emotions onto other people. But if you are the leader of a team, and you are struggling with something for whatever reason, it could be personal. It could be work-related. To what extent can you share that with your team? You don't have to share all of the details of your situation, but can you let them know that you are dealing with something difficult at the moment, so you may not be yourself, you may not be reacting in the way you normally would. If you show them courage and vulnerability, they are more encouraged to do the same with you and let you know when something might be troubling them.

Some might ask why this matters, if not from a human to human perspective; from a risk perspective, law firms need to know when people are struggling and might be more likely to miss something or make an error of judgment.

This is going to be so important as we build the new post-pandemic. Rather than people try and put their heads down and get on with everything, assume business as usual, which has always been a problem in law, leading to increased stress and anxiety. If people feel that they can come to their leader and share how they're feeling and that maybe they need a little bit of support, then we're going to get through this next phase.

In our post-pandemic world, we're going to need great leaders. We need those who can learn not to fear vulnerability and genuine open connection. These skills are going to become vitally important, not being afraid of emotions, being able to talk to team members about how they're feeling, are they struggling with the changes, and what the future holds?

Personally, having been on this journey for a few years, is that the more open and vulnerable you can be with people (in the right situations using your common sense, of course), this creates a better and a stronger connection, whether it's with your clients, your peers at work or new contacts in a networking sense. This vulnerability and connection piece allows you to stand out compared to others. This is why I refer to Authenticity as a Lawyer's Superpower!

Many lawyers will be too afraid to show any signs of emotion, vulnerability, or compassion to open up and be who they truly are with other people. Those who do will stand out from everyone else, whether it's in a leadership role, as part of a team, or whether it's in a business development/networking sense.

I asked Trevor Sterling (Senior Partner at Moore Barlow) what support leaders needed from their organisations in order to be really great in their role.

"You've got to allow me to, to remain me, Trevor Sterling, and not become some clone of the business. Because my individuality is my personality, and without personality you lose a lot. Personality is really, really important, and that comes from having a whole diverse range of people within your business.

The the ability to be me is really important. That's the one thing I need from any firm, and that is to allow me to be myself, bring my authentic self into the workplace, and allow my personality as my authentic self to shine through, because I am different.
And that difference is good."

Chapter 10

Change and the Future

"The best way to predict the
future is to create it."

– THEODORE HOOK

As we've seen in the Culture in Law Chapter, and as no doubt, you've probably experienced yourself first hand, there are a lot of issues facing the legal profession. How many of us would choose law a second time if we had our time again? How many of us would want our children to go into this career?

Attrition rates

We need to tackle the high numbers of lawyers leaving the profession, especially around the 5 to 10-year point - as they can't reconcile the profession with their vision for their life. After years of study, hard work, and dedication, we shouldn't be losing these lawyers. We should be flexible and adaptable enough to have room or perhaps even to welcome everyone who has worked so hard to get there with open arms.

That is not to say that the law doesn't prepare us for lots of second careers. It most certainly does! I always prefer that those who choose to leave do so from a position of control and personal choice rather than feeling that they have no other option.

As we embrace more and more of our own authenticity, we can find that the environment we work in, the clients we work with, or even the area in which we practise doesn't fit with us anymore. I've seen this with a client who, in his early 50s, began to question what the rest of his career looked like.

He'd spent years working for large plc companies, and as he started to explore more about his life and his own personal values, he began to discover that he'd let go of his love for the environment, nature, and wildlife. He actually worked for companies that actively destroyed these things in the name of progress and profit. Now he didn't up and quit his job, but he decided to reduce his hours a little to spend more time on his passions outside work.

We can't always love our work, and quitting at that moment is rarely an option. But we can explore (maybe remind ourselves of) our old passions, what lights us up, what makes us – us.

I like to think that we will see increasing numbers of lawyers rejecting what has been the previously accepted pattern of long working hours, and very little by way of outside life interests. (And I originally wrote that comment pre-pandemic!)

There is a familiar pattern among those who work long hours during the week and then feel a sense of guilt at the weekend if they do anything other than dedicate themselves to the family. This pattern keeps us firmly on the treadmill or the profession conveyor belt. When does that person have any time for themselves?

I "should" be able to fix it

We are trained to be problem solvers and look for problems in the first place. It's what we're paid to spend all day doing. So when it comes to our mental health and even our enjoyment of our work, we think we should be able to fix it.

When I speak to lawyers on the brink of burnout or already mid depression or anxiety, they will frequently share the belief that they should be able to fix this themselves. This belief stops them from reaching out for support earlier. I like to think that this might be changing; it's certainly part of my mission to continue raising awareness and having these important conversations.

It's not a weakness or a failure to reach out for help. In fact, it's a strength, and we emerge stronger as a result.

Lawyerpreneurs

What are lawyerpreneurs?

It's not about thinking outside the box; haven't we been doing that since our first training contract interviews? It's about throwing the box out of the window and starting all over again.

We need to not think like lawyers. We need to look to other industries and disciplines outside of our own if we want to find new solutions. But more importantly, we need to do that as our authentic real, and best selves, not who we think we should be. We are not simply cookie-cutter replicas of the people who have trained us. Our knowledge and legal skills are a given. What is the extra over and above the legal know-how that makes the lawyerpreneur what and who we are? Passionate about what we care about and what we stand for. We see past the legal issues; they are merely in the background.

The distinctive traits of the lawyerpreneur are leadership, inspiration, vision, compassion, inclusivity, innovation, and bravery.

Lawyerpreneurs might be running their own business, or they may be operating inside a firm. It doesn't matter – they are the leaders who think differently and do things differently, usually right outside their comfort zone, where the magic happens.

What does this have to do with authenticity?

In my mind, those lawyers who embrace authenticity as a superpower, who take the steps towards being more of themselves in everything they do, will be the natural leaders and lawyerpreneurs of the future.

When we're being authentic, we can't help but be driven by our own values, vision, and aspirations for our own future, the future of the profession, and perhaps even the world?

On a podcast with Ryan Holtz, I recently heard that we couldn't reach our potential unless we were our full authentic selves living a life of purpose. By exploring our authentic selves, we can't help but begin to discover our purpose and then live it

To be truly authentic pretty much demands it.

Leadership is a natural step for authentic lawyerpreneurs. Good leaders embody trust, honesty, openness, compassion, and being authentic. They may be leaders in name, team leader, CEO etc., but perhaps they are not. They lead by example; they may lead peers, and even guide senior colleagues and those that will come after them.

Inspiring others is similarly a byproduct of becoming more authentic. While taking the first steps towards authenticity might be daunting and easily avoided through fear of judgment or rejection, all of life becomes easier once embraced. When I deliver my favourite keynote presentation on Authenticity as a Lawyer's Superpower and talk about dropping the mask and character armour, relief and possibility are palpable.

Being in this career without the mask and armour naturally inspires others to follow your example. Whilst we don't want cookie-cutter carbon copies, if others are inspired to discover their own authenticity and the courage to live this, we've really made a difference and maybe helped create future leaders.

A part of discovering who we really are involves inquiring into our role here, our legacy, what we stand for, and what difference we will make? For me, it's being part of changing the culture in law. This book is just a part of that mission. In 2016 at a business retreat in Scotland, I set that mission as my 10-year vision. It seemed ridiculous or impossible, but now it's a reality. I don't do it alone. I hold that vision for the future, talk about it, and find myself surrounded by others who feel the same. Together will bring about that change to the culture in law.

Our authentic selves have a vision for a better future for ourselves, our families, our teams, and indeed our whole profession. In the noise and business of our careers, we stop listening to the voice that has something important to say. Tapping into our authentic self, listening to that little voice, reminds us of our vision of what really matters to us. In becoming more authentic, we can't help but start working towards it and bring others along with us.

When I started writing this book in 2019, the change I expected to be talking about involved a greater awareness of stress and mental health and the impact that it has on lawyers and, consequently, the profession; how it was certainly my hope that in the coming years' stress would no longer just be accepted as part and parcel of the job and something that we all had to get on with.

But in the meantime, the world has gone through a period of change in a way that none of us expected. Whilst the pandemic affected everyone, I've followed its impact on the legal profession with great interest and a lot of hope.

As no doubt you picked up throughout this book, I have always been a proponent for more working from home, more flexibility, more agile working, and more autonomy for the legal profession. This way of working is more conducive to work-life balance, reducing stress, and improving physical and mental health.

But importantly, productivity has increased, and law firm profitability has increased throughout the pandemic (despite the challenges of homeschooling, feelings of isolation, and working in sometimes not ideal environments).

This proves my original point very nicely – greater flexibility and autonomy will result in improved well-being and higher productivity.

During the first lockdown, I had a very timely conversation with business psychologist Matt Smeed. We discussed whether or not our values had changed as a result of the pandemic. It might be believed that earlier generations had different values. Perhaps they valued family, home, and security more than we have done. It appeared that we tended toward valuing achievement, promotion, status, or wealth. I think the pandemic has given us all an opportunity to re-evaluate what's important to us, and for many, the values of home, family, and health have really come to the forefront of their mind.

Whether this is a change in values or, as I suspect, a realisation of what's important, I'm not sure this is something that can be undone. I would like to think the legal profession has changed for the better in that whilst our firms and businesses need to be profitable, effective, and successful, the way to do this is to look after the mental health, well-being, and happiness of the lawyers.

In terms of who's responsible for mental health and well-being, in my opinion, it's 50% the firm and 50% the individual. I also live in great hope that lawyers who have found a more balanced lifestyle will not be so ready to give this up in the future or to go back to the way things were.

You and Your Future

Because you're reading this book, I'm going to guess that you don't necessarily think like the vast majority of our profession, or certainly the way we have thought in the past. I believe we are in a time of great change for many of the reasons already set out in this book. Younger generations of lawyers in much larger numbers want something different.

Money and status aren't necessarily their driving force; they want to make a difference; they want purpose, fulfilment, and work-life balance. Some of us older lawyers want these things too, even more so since the pandemic.

But it's not about choosing between achievement and balance or between money and happiness. I learned this when I stopped working crazy hours, learned to delegate and trust others, and spent time doing more of what I was really good at.

IT IS POSSIBLE to have success on your terms AND the work-life harmony you're looking for.

Is it necessarily easy? No.
Can it happen overnight? Rarely.
But is it worth it? Always.

I sincerely hope this book and the accompanying website resources will be a step on your journey to creating more of what you want for your life.

About the Author

Hi I'm Hannah, and yes, I am a commercial property lawyer! I am also a 3 x business owner, coach & trainer to the legal profession, speaker, podcast host, author, wife of very patient Nick, and a proud Mum of three amazing boys, Teddy, Rufus, and Victor.

It's been a privilege to share my story and thoughts with you inside this book, and I would love to hear from you about what has impacted you the most, what are you seeing differently now, and importantly, how will this change your life and career; for the better going forward?

Other Books and Services by the Author

You can find out more about my coaching and training work at www.authenticallyspeaking.co.uk.

Don't forget to register your copy of this book and access all of the additional resources at www.theauthenticlawyer.com

Please do also connect with me on Linkedin where I share details of events and networking groups.
https://www.linkedin.com/in/hannahbeko/

Printed in Great Britain
by Amazon

22637387R00116